PRAISE FOR *THE SCHOOLS WE NEED NOW*

The Schools We Need Now *resonates deeply with the challenges and responsibilities we face in nurturing students in today's schools. This insightful guide offers a crucial perspective, emphasizing the paramount importance of addressing social and emotional concepts during this pivotal stage of students' cognitive development. It serves as an invaluable tool for administrators, providing practical strategies to guide our school communities toward creating environments that prioritize mental health. As a founding principal of a middle school that opened in July 2022, I highly encourage others to utilize this must-read roadmap for fostering positive, supportive spaces where young minds flourish and thrive.*
—**Anne Marie Adkins**, *Middle School Principal, NC*

Each day, headlines about devastating mental health issues in schools for students and staff grab our attention. The impact is far-reaching. Better mental health strategies and supports make a lifetime of difference for everyone—sometimes a life and death difference. Drs. Tim Dohrer and Tom Golebiewski have lived and studied all aspects of mental health in the school setting. They are experienced in real schoolhouse issues, have researched best practices, and have led powerful, meaningful, and practical professional development for many years. The key elements that differentiate these authors are their authentic experiences, leadership, and passion for strengthening mental health in our schools.

—**Maureen Cheever, PhD**, *Senior Professional Learning Director, Illinois Principals Association*

This book is a paradigm-shifting way to truly understand how to implement the Mental Health Action Plan in K-12 schools. The comprehensive step-by-step approach addresses the development model for the whole child that is so critical to designing mentally healthier schools in this country. It's a road map to transformational change!

—**Sabrina P. Gracias**, *Founder, Ortus Foundation*

This book ensures that educators have systems and practices in place to support the mental health needs of students. It is a gold mine, packed with reflective questions for school teams to discuss while developing or revising their school plans. It provides many examples of student cases, recent data, and strategies that can be implemented immediately.

—**Jessica Johnson**, *District Administrator,*
Dodgeland School District, WI

One of the biggest challenges school leaders face is the mental health crisis we're dealing with in schools around the world. Facing such a huge challenge, we can feel overwhelmed by all we need to do. This book gives people exactly what they need, so they can meet the crisis head on and come up with positive, powerful solutions.

—**Jim Knight**, *Founder and Senior Partner,*
Instructional Coaching Group, Author of
High-Impact Instruction

This is the right book at the right time. Schools are struggling to support students and families who are in crisis and those who are just trying to manage the demands that have led to increased stress and depression, social media addiction, and increased loneliness and isolation. We have to do more and better for our students, and this book provides very helpful templates and suggestions that are actionable immediately.

—**Marianne L. Lescher**, *K-8 School Principal,*
Kyrene School District, AZ

The Schools We Need Now *offers a practical and holistic approach to fostering mental well-being in schools. The authors have masterfully distilled the complex and ever-evolving landscape of mental health support within an educational context into a clear, actionable, and accessible roadmap. This book serves as a quick and comprehensive guide that is both informative and user-friendly, making it an invaluable asset for educators, administrators, and support staff alike.*

—**Debra Paradowski**, *Associate Principal,*
Arrowhead Union High School, WI

While navigating the adolescent years involves some universal developmental experiences for all individuals, we know that each student brings their own experiences, identities, strengths, and challenges to these transformative years. The same can be said for their families, educators, and communities. While we learn from the past and current best practices, we also have an obligation to understand how we can create the schools of the future; those that are designed to be dynamic learning communities of possibilities, joy, and unlimited growth for all. The Schools We Need Now *by Tim Dohrer and Tom Golebiewski is an inclusive* and collaborative guide that all community stakeholder groups can use to actively engage in the creation of a mentally healthy school and to use proactive design strategies and a practical roadmap to develop a school where every student, regardless of background or learning style, can thrive.

—**Miriam Pike**, *Head of School, Wolcott College Prep High School, IL*

In "The Schools We Need Now: A Guide to Designing a Mentally Healthy School," Timothy Dohrer and Thomas Golebiewski brilliantly blend their extensive expertise in education and mental health to advocate for a transformative perspective on school environments. Their approach, deeply rooted in both classic educational philosophies and contemporary scholarship, emphasizes mental health as an integral, rather than peripheral, component of educational systems. The authors' commitment to this vision is evident through their engaging narrative, offering readers practical, reflective exercises that seamlessly blend mental wellness with educational content. As a clinical social worker, scholar, and youth suicide prevention expert, I find their reframing of schools through a mental health lens both compelling and necessary, offering a fresh, inclusive viewpoint that will resonate with educators of varied experiences and backgrounds. This concise, insightful book not only challenges the status quo but also equips its readers with the understanding and tools to envision and cultivate schools where mental health is at the heart of education.

—**Jonathan B. Singer, PhD, LCSW**
Professor, Loyola University Chicago, School of Social WorkCoauthor of Suicide in Schools: A Practitioner's Guide to Multilevel Prevention, Assessment, Intervention and Postvention

In these challenging post-pandemic times, Dohrer and Golebiewski provide leadership in rethinking one of our highest priority social and school improvement topics: the mental health of America's youth. They offer a comprehensive treatment of this complex domain, including the current social context of mental health, visions of excellence, and priority needs and how to meet them. Their work arises from exceptional scholarship combined with a thoughtful sense of practical reality. This book offers a roadmap to student mental and academic well-being.

—**Rick Stiggins**, *Author,* Give Our Student the Gift of Confidence

In their informative and instructive book, Tim Dohrer and Tom Golebiewski have accurately identified the mental health crisis that all schools are experiencing in the post-pandemic era. This current reality necessitates establishing a supportive, inclusive, and equitable school community for students, their families, and their teachers.

The Schools We Need Now *calls us to rethink the purpose of schooling and learning. We must attend to students' social and psychological well-being along with their academic progress. We must prioritize child, adolescent, and adult development and adopt pedagogy that addresses the whole child and culturally responsive teaching. We must understand social and emotional learning domains that create a school culture of care, belonging, and wellness and we must embrace assessment for learning rather than assessment of learning. We must include family mental health education programs and services. Finally, we must create conditions, systems, and structures that maximize support, prevention, intervention, and trauma-informed teaching practices.* The Schools We Need Now *provides a blueprint to create a multi-tiered school-based mental health action plan that considers childhood trauma, stress, anxiety, grief, loss, transitions, and self-harm.*

—**Richard Streedain,** *Leadership Coach, Common Foundation*

THE SCHOOLS
WE NEED NOW

THE SCHOOLS WE NEED NOW

A Guide to Designing a Mentally Healthy School

TIMOTHY DOHRER

THOMAS GOLEBIEWSKI

Foreword by David Adams

For information:

Corwin
A Sage Company
2455 Teller Road
Thousand Oaks, California 91320
(800) 233-9936
www.corwin.com

Sage Publications Ltd.
1 Oliver's Yard
55 City Road
London EC1Y 1SP
United Kingdom

Sage Publications India Pvt. Ltd.
Unit No 323-333, Third Floor, F-Block
International Trade Tower Nehru Place
New Delhi 110 019
India

Sage Publications Asia-Pacific Pte. Ltd.
18 Cross Street #10-10/11/12
China Square Central
Singapore 048423

Printed in the United States of America

Paperback ISBN 978-1-0719-2394-8

This book is printed on acid-free paper.

Vice President and Editorial Director: Monica Eckman
Publisher: Jessica Allan
Content Development Editor: Mia Rodriguez
Senior Editorial Assistant: Natalie Delpino
Production Editor: Vijayakumar
Copy Editor: Diane DiMura
Typesetter: TNQ Tech Pvt. Ltd.
Proofreader: Girish Sharma
Indexer: TNQ Tech Pvt. Ltd.
Cover Designer: Gail Buschman
Marketing Manager: Olivia Bartlett

24 25 26 27 28 10 9 8 7 6 5 4 3 2 1

CONTENTS

Foreword by David Adams   xiii

Acknowledgments   xvii

About the Authors   xix

1. The Need for Mentally Healthy Schools   1
   Why Is Mental Health Important in Schools?   2
   Tom's Positionality   4
   Tim's Positionality   5
   Our Work Together   6
   Creating a Mental Health Action Plan   7
   Your Context and Positionality   7
   Overview of the Book and Your Plan   8
   What Could This Look Like?   9
   A Call to Action   12
   Creating Your Mental Health Action Plan: A Template   13

2. Mental Health and Mental Models   15
   Mental Model: A Developmental Model for the Whole Child   17
   Mental Model: A Whole-School Systems Thinking Approach   20
   Mental Model: A Culture of Caring   23
   Mental Model: A Continuum of Care   25
   Mental Model: Thinking Differently About Mental Health   27
   Mental Model: A Multitiered Systems of Support Approach to
      Mental Health   28
   Conclusion: Mental Models as the Foundation of Your Action Plan   30
   Creating Your Mental Health Action Plan   32

3. Tier 1 Mental Health: Universal Supports for All   37
   Tier 1: What Do We Mean by "Universal"?   38
   Tier 1 as Prevention and Early Intervention   39
   Universal Challenges to Everyone   41
   Safety First: "Maslow Before You Bloom"   41
   Stigma and Stereotypes   43

Disconnection From Relationships and Community   44
Identity   45
Diversity, Equity, and Inclusion   46
Environmental Risk and Protective Factors   47
Technology and Social Media   48
Tier 1 Interventions   49
Everything Rests on the Foundation of Tier 1   60
Creating Your Mental Health Action Plan   62

4. Tier 2 Issues and Interventions for Students, Teachers, and
   Parents ... and Schools!   67
   Tier 1 and Tier 2 Screeners: Building an Early Detection System   68
   Internalized Behaviors: Stress, Anxiety, and Trauma   70
   Related Tier 2 Issues: Loneliness, Isolation, Grief, and Loss   80
   Tier 2 Interventions and Strategies   82
   Mindfulness in Schools   84
   Circles   85
   Student Behavior and Discipline: A Shift to Restorative Practices   89
   Trauma-Informed Practice   92
   Small Groups   93
   Peer Helping, Mediation, Mentoring, and Tutoring   94
   Anti-Bullying Programs   95
   Student Activities and Clubs   96
   Parent/Family Education, Programs, and Engagement   97
   A Healthy and Well-Regulated Staff   98
   Final Thoughts   100
   Creating Your Mental Health Action Plan   101

5. Tier 3: Supporting Students and Staff With the Greatest Needs   105
   Defining Tier 3 and How It Connects to Tiers 1 and 2   106
   Defining Mental Illness   108
   Comorbidity   110
   Anxiety and Depression   111
   School Refusal   113
   Transitions   114
   Substance Use   115
   Disordered Eating   117
   Focus on Self-Harm   117
   Suicidal Ideation   118
   Suicide   120
   Suicide Intervention   121
   Focus on Disruptive Behavior Disorders   123
   Childhood Trauma   124

Equity and Mental Illness   127
Focus on Neurodiversity   128
Tier 3 Prevention and Intervention   129
Concluding Thoughts   137
Creating Your Mental Health Action Plan   139

6. Integrating the Mental Health Action Plan in Your School   143
Begin With Belonging   144
Rethinking the Organization of a School   145
Rethinking the Physical Building   147
Rethinking Technology and Mental Health   149
Rethinking Curriculum, Instruction, and Assessment   150
Rethinking Teachers and Instruction   151
Rethinking Assessment   152
Rethinking Transitions   153
Rethinking After-School Activities   156
Rethinking School Context and Community Assets   157
Implementing a Comprehensive Mental Health Action Plan   160
A School That Is Changing the Game: Wolcott College
    Prep High School   162
Conclusion   164
Creating Your Mental Health Action Plan   166

Appendix A: Mental Health Action Plan   171
Index   185

Visit the companion website at
www.schoolsweneednow.com
for downloadable resources.

FOREWORD

I'm an educator at heart and the educators among us know that there is nothing like a great analogy. So, when I was preparing to write this foreword, I went looking for inspiration to better understand how to construct environments where students felt connected, the kind of environment that the recommendations in this book promotes. In short, I went searching for the perfect analogy, and as I scoured literature from psychology to chemistry, I kept finding a recurring theme: bonds matter.

This idea that elements, atoms, and people are driven to connect in order to find an equilibrium is reflected in everything from attachment theory to our most fundamental physics. The more I kept searching, the clearer it became that I could learn a lot from the natural world about the nature of bonds and how they inform our common sense of purpose.

Let's take hydrogen, one of the most abundant elements in the universe and one of the most eager to bond. Left alone, hydrogen is extremely reactive, its single electron sensitive to any opportunity to create a more stable energy configuration. Hydrogen wants to connect. In fact, hydrogen is so eager to bond that some of the world's most interesting resources have hydrogen to thank for their existence. Hydrocarbons, including fuels like gasoline, are hydrogen compounds. Hydrogen peroxide helps disinfect wounds. And of course, the best-known hydrogen compound, H_2O, is the source of all life: water.

It's not all positive though. Hydrogen also bonds with chlorine to make hydrochloric acid, a strong acid known for its corrosive nature and its ability to break down everything from metals to food in our stomach. Useful, but dangerous. So, it's hydrogen's eagerness to bond that puts it into relationships with many other elements, with the resulting compounds manifesting new and exciting properties that have shaped the universe we live in…and I would be remiss if I didn't mention that one of the most stable hydrogen compounds is when hydrogen is in relationship with itself: H_2.

But you didn't pick up this book for a chemistry lesson. This is a book about school mental health and what educators can do to elevate it for our youth.

One of the defining aspects of adolescence is a shift towards peer groups and away from adults. Our teens are hydrogen atoms eager to bond. The quality of those bonds and their resulting relationships can serve ultimately as risk or protective factors for our students' mental health. It depends on what our students bond to.

Let's first think through our students' relationship with themselves (H_2). In the language of social-emotional learning, this bond is achieved through the domains of self-awareness, the ability to understand who we are, what we need, and how we feel relative to the world around us, and self-management, the ability to manage one's behavior in prosocial ways.

In the domain of self-awareness students excel when they are provided with learning experiences, models, and feedback that result in their ability to demonstrate:

- awareness of their needs and emotions;
- awareness of their personal traits, strengths, and opportunities for growth;
- awareness of their external supports;
- a sense of personal responsibility;
- hopefulness and positive expectations regarding themselves and their abilities in the present and future.

Self-awareness helps facilitate self-management, where students excel when they are provided opportunities that result in their ability to demonstrate:

- the ability to manage one's needs and emotions;
- the use of effective choice-making and decision-making skills;
- increasing levels of independence and the ability to set and achieve goals.

Through these learning experiences, students develop the ability to relate to themselves in constructive ways, paving the way for the type of diatomic bond that leads to strong mental health: the bond with oneself. Schools are a crucial space for this work to happen by teaching students about their emotions, modeling coping skills, and elevating thinking strategies that promote a sense of efficacy and optimism. This is "emotional learning." This is the work of our schools, and this is the foundation of mental health.

However, the true strength of the hydrogen atom emerges from its bonds with others.

Recall that chemical compounds form in order to increase the stability of each of the separate elements. We like to think humans are enormously complex beings – and we are – but not so complex that we can't relate with the humble hydrogen atom, seeking relationships that foster stability in ourselves and others. In the context of social-emotional learning, our ability to relate to others is captured in the domains of social awareness, or students' awareness of the role and value of others in the greater community, and social management, which is students' ability to interact with others in meaningful and productive ways. Specifically, within domain of social awareness students excel when they are provided with learning experiences, models, and feedback that result in their ability to demonstrate:

- awareness of other people's roles, their emotions and perspectives;
- consideration for others and a desire to positively contribute to their community;
- the ability to respond to and read social or pertinent environmental cues.

And in social management when they have opportunities that result in their ability to:

- demonstrate positive communication and social skills to interact effectively with others;
- develop constructive relationships;
- prevent, manage, and resolve interpersonal conflicts in constructive ways.

The social domain – how students bond to others – is a critical space for schools to invest. Everything from instructional strategies to extracurricular activities to direct instruction help students develop the skills to manage relationships and cement the bonds that will promote mental health and serve as protective factors when our young people struggle. This is "social learning."

By integrating the domains of self and social, enhancing the competencies of awareness and management, and offering learning experiences for our students, schools create opportunities for students to engage effectively in "social and emotional learning."

Social-emotional skills and school climate have a bidirectional relationship, with students' (and adults') ability to relate to others constructively helping create a climate where social problem-solving is valued and a sense of belonging is fostered. This belonging, our perceptions of the bonds that help create stability in ourselves and others, is a crucial factor in students' mental health. And educators can foster it.

There's no perfect analogy, but my journey to find one has taught me that whether it's the microcosmic interactions of hydrogen atoms or the expansive relationships of human beings, this fundamental truth remains: connections define existence. "The Schools We Need Now: A Guide to Designing a Mentally Healthy School" is a book that's focused on practical ways to structure schools that build the inter- and intra-personal connections students need to thrive. Authors Tim Dohrer and Tom Golebiewski invite us to pause and reflect: What data are we collecting to understand our students' strengths and challenges in the social emotional domain? What protective factors and existing structures are available to promote connection and problem-solving? What routines can be incorporated to drive belonging? In what ways are we preparing our teachers to support our students' social, emotional, and academic development?

The principles that drive atoms to seek out stability through bonds are not so different from the social and emotional ties that shape our lives and mental well-being, and as educators we hold a key to shaping these connections. This book prepares us to do just that, because from the atomic to the human level, in every sense of the word, bonds matter.

David Adams
Chief Executive Officer
The Urban Assembly
New York, NY

ACKNOWLEDGMENTS

While this text is a culmination of our combined experiences over the past 40 years, we began imagining the book in 2013 in a coffee shop in Evanston, Illinois. We are deeply thankful for the hundreds of people who have walked with us to envision schools that center mental health. Early on, we had incredible support from the Illinois Principals Association, especially Jean Smith, Maureen Cheever, Sue Holmes, Beth Broyles, Arlin Peebles, and Jason Leahy. Dick Streedain, one of the first administrators to manage a school shooting in a U.S. school, spurred us on to "tell our story" and introduced us to Rick Stiggins, who connected us to Corwin Press. We want to thank our colleagues at New Trier High School, Wolcott College Prep, Northwestern University, Northern Illinois University, the School of Social Work at Loyola University of Chicago, and the Institute for Clinical Social Work. Much of this book was written and edited at the Mount Prospect Public Library as well as various places across the country from California to South Carolina! Thanks for graphic design by Jane Tomlinson. The editors at Corwin Press have been wonderful to us and have a deep regard for wellness as a priority in schools and life. Thanks so much to Jessica Allan, Natalie Delpino, Mia Rodriguez, and Lucas Schleicher.

We conducted dozens of interviews as background for the book and deeply thank them all for spending time sharing their stories, including the following: Anne Marie Adkins, Jesse DiMartino, Annya Artigas, Sara Banks, Katie Conklin, Brandon Combs, Peggy Kubert, Johanna Jacobson, Karen Foley, Jamon Flowers, Jeff McLellan, Arlene Messner-Peters, Lisa Mullaney, Stephanie Nolen, Miriam Pike, Lani Potts, Kay Pranis, Ryan Redman, Meg Rondenet, Alec Ross, Jodie Siegal, Jonathan Singer, Dick Streedain, and Addie Van Zwoll.

So much of the work any of us does that really matters is because of our past and current relationships. Both of us learned from amazing mentors and colleagues such as Bernie Lifson, Jan Borja, Tim Hayes, Josh Seldess, Matt Ottaviano, John Cadwell, Alison Gordon, Miriam Pike, Ed Dunkleblau, Maurice Elias, Roger Weissberg, Tom Garden, Joan Gross, Lou Gross, Seth Harkins, Jim Wolters, Diane Juneau, Jon White, Solomon Cytrynbaum, Elan Adler, Mary Deignan, Ellen Kenemore, and the English and Social Work departments at New Trier High School.

Each of us have been deeply impacted by the thousands of students and educators we have worked with over the decades. Their stories fill this book. Finally, both our immediate and extended families not only supported us but provided the reason for placing mental health front and center in our work. From Tim, I dedicate this book to my parents, Larry and Paula, who have always been so proud of my work as an educator, and to the amazing gals in my life: Stephanie, Catherine, Rebecca, and Elizabeth. From Tom, I dedicate this book to my inspiring, loving, and supportive wife, Gretchen; children Jane, Thomas, William, and their spouses, Joe, Amber, and Madelyn; my grandchildren, Caroline, Eleanor, Charlie, John, Ada, Odin, and Sophia.

PUBLISHER'S ACKNOWLEDGMENT

Corwin gratefully acknowledges the contributions of the following reviewers:

Amanda Austin
Principal
Iberville Parish School Board
Plaquemine, Louisiana

Jessica Johnson
District Administrator
Dodgeland School District
Juneau, WI

Marianne L. Lescher, PhD
K–8 School Principal
Kyrene School District
Chandler, AZ

Debra Paradowski
Associate Principal
Arrowhead Union High School
Hartland, WI

Karen L. Tichy, EdD
Assistant Professor of Educational Leadership
Saint Louis University
St Louis, MO

ABOUT THE AUTHORS

Dr. Timothy Dohrer has been a classroom teacher, administrator, and consultant for over 30 years in K–12 schools and higher education. He was a teacher and principal at New Trier High School in Winnetka, Illinois, a school of 4,000 students and staff. He has also served as a director and assistant professor at Northwestern University and Northern Illinois University, and an adjunct instructor at Pennsylvania State University and Northeastern Illinois University. Tim continues to serve on a variety of boards and regularly consults with schools in and around Chicago and Illinois. Tim's major areas of research include social and emotional learning, school climate, curriculum theory, teacher education, and leadership. He has BAs in English and journalism from Indiana University, an MA in English from Northwestern University, and a PhD in curriculum and instruction from Pennsylvania State University.

Dr. Thomas Golebiewski is a licensed clinical social worker. He has worked in schools for 40 years, including 26 years as department chair of social work at New Trier High School in Winnetka, Illinois. Tom has served as an adjunct professor at University of Chicago's School of Social Service Administration, Northwestern University's School of Education and Social Policy, and currently at Loyola University of Chicago School of Social Work, where he is also an internship liaison. He has a private practice in psychotherapy, counseling and consultation in Wilmette, Illinois, and is currently a consultant at Wolcott College Prep, an independent school in Chicago. Tom also volunteers as a Red Cross disaster mental health responder, has been a board member at A Safe Place, Lake County, Illinois, and the Mental Health Association of the North Shore. He is a state-appointed committee member of the Illinois Domestic Violence Fatality Review Commission, and the Lake County Family Violence Coordinating Council. He is on the program steering committee and a regular presenter for the Naomi Ruth Cohen Institute annual conference that addresses mental health. Dr. Golebiewski received his BA and MSW from Loyola University in Chicago and a PhD in clinical social work from The Institute for Clinical Social Work in Chicago.

CHAPTER 1

....

THE NEED FOR MENTALLY HEALTHY SCHOOLS

Education is not preparation for life; education is life itself.
—Dewey, 1916

At the beginning of 2020, schools in the United States were already close to a breaking point in dealing with a tidal wave of mental health issues affecting kids. Young people in greater and greater numbers were being diagnosed with mental disorders and facing increasing levels of stress, anxiety, and trauma. Organizations like the National Alliance for Mental Illness (NAMI) reported that one in six young people in the United States were experiencing a mental health disorder, but only about half of them were receiving any kind of treatment (National Alliance for Mental Illness [NAMI], 2019). The Centers for Disease Control (CDC, 2022) warned that suicide was the second leading cause of death among teens and young adults.

Then the COVID-19 global pandemic hit.

The pandemic not only exposed the issues plaguing American schools, it doubled and amplified the problems. By 2022, 79% of psychologists reported seeing a dramatic increase in the number of patients with anxiety and depression symptoms, with the largest increase among patients ages 18 to 25 (American Psychological Association [APA], 2022). "The national mental health crisis continues," said Arthur Evans, CEO of the American Psychological Association. The annual Mental Health America Survey found an increase in suicidal ideation and young people experiencing a major depressive episode over the previous year's data (Mental Health Association [MHA], 2022). Clearly, the pandemic exacerbated an already overwhelming mental health crisis.

On the front lines of working with kids, teachers, administrators, and school staff have been clamoring for support and changes to help kids in need of mental and physical wellness. After decades of focusing on academic achievement and standardized test scores, more and more educators and Americans are seeing the need to rethink our approach to schooling and place mental health at the very center of how we educate kids and operate schools.

This book is a clarion call to do just that. We are offering a new, post-pandemic vision for schooling that impacts all stakeholders: students, educators, parents, and communities. It is based on science, decades of research, and proven examples from educators across the country. It's also something the two of us have been promoting for over a decade in hopes of remaking schools into safer, more relational places to live, learn, and work.

One of the things that keeps bringing the two of us together in our work is a shared vision for the purpose of schools. A school is a learning organization that brings people together across our shared, democratic culture so they can develop academically, socially, emotionally, and physically. On a practical level, it is a safe place that holds and protects kids in loco parentis so adults in the family can pursue their own goals like careers, higher education, and self-improvement. A school is also an important organization within a community, serving as a reflection of local values as well as a collaborator with members of that community.

If we begin to unpack that definition of schools, we see that our vision of schools is not about changing some of the core functions that have been in place for decades. In fact, some of these core functions helped students navigate the COVID-19 pandemic, as well as the recent social and political crises. We have learned the importance of having an adult mentor, connecting with peers, experiencing structure and routine, accessing health and wellness services, technology, supplies, and extracurricular activities. And like museums and libraries, schools play a crucial role in our society in providing knowledge, promoting culture, and making space for dialog, discussion, and debate. These functions need to continue, but they need to take mental health into consideration from the start. By doing so, we could improve schools beyond where they are today.

WHY IS MENTAL HEALTH IMPORTANT IN SCHOOLS?

Much has been written about mental health through a variety of perspectives: medical models, deficit models, prevention models, holistic approaches, systems perspectives, and transactional models. Each comes with core values and an underlying framework of guiding principles and claims. Given these models and the demands facing schools, pivotal questions must be asked that can help us come up with new systems and strategies for helping kids. What matters most in education today? What can be done for all of our students not only to learn but to thrive? How do we make school healthy places for all to learn?

What Schools Due to Address Mental Health Matters

Mental health should be embedded in a school's mission, policies, practices, and programs. Surrounding that focus should be social and emotional and physical safety, risk and protective factors, supportive relationships, restorative justice, and mental health education programs. Schools should also focus on prevention activities, transition planning, crisis response, and community and family collaborations (see Figure 1.1). By placing mental health at the center of our thinking and our work, school leaders approach all those other aspects of schooling from a different perspective.

FIGURE 1.1   MENTAL HEALTH AT THE CENTER OF THE SCHOOL

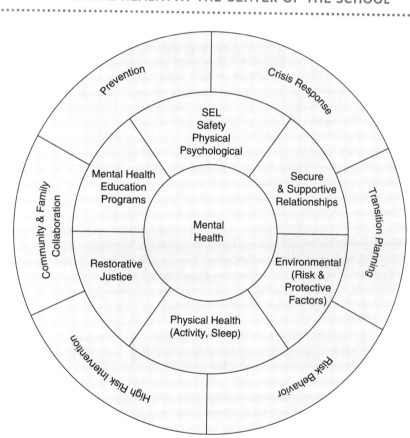

SOURCE: Illustration by Jane Tomlinson.

Each school should have a comprehensive Mental Health Action Plan that is grounded in its culture and climate and just about everything that it does. Such a plan would comprehensively use a multitiered system of support (MTSS), have a holistic approach to people and learning, focus on community partnerships, and create a "continuum of care" where social and emotional support and protective factors align to build capacity, increase assets, reduce risk, and cultivate resilience.

Although many schools are developing policies and initiatives, the time calls for clarity of purpose and vision in considering mental health issues in schools. We need to think beyond deficit and medical models of mental illness to ones that are transactional and take into account multiple domains of functioning and well-being (Sameroff, 2009). Much of our understanding of mental health is based upon medical models like the *DSM-5*, which is a classification system to identify problems, assigning a label to internal pathological conditions. This medical model focuses upon internal factors with less attention to sociocultural and economic factors. Each school has its own organizational culture and structure. Therefore, each school must have its own approach to mental health that is contextual and local. Just as we should take a holistic approach to working with individual students, we need to take a holistic approach to working with schools.

When people think of mental health they often think of illness (a deficit model) and clinical therapeutic interventions (a medical model). But to think more broadly, mental health in schools promotes healthy development; considers multiple domains of cognitive, social, and emotional functioning; takes into account the prevention of psychosocial problems like bullying, substance use abuse, and school violence; and cultivates protective factors while minimizing risk. We need to develop a "Continuum of Care" that considers prevention and early intervention, builds capacities, and allows systems to foster mental health of its school community, including students, staff, families, and parents.

To move beyond a deficit or medical model is to take into consideration a more transformational framework that is holistic and centers the whole child in a partnership between parents and community and school. It takes into account contexts, history, power, and possibility, framing a vision of what schools can be like when focusing on the mental health of all members of its community. It embeds social and emotional learning, cultural humility, systems thinking, and equity. This can start by looking critically and deeply at who we are and where we come from, something known as *positionality*. By identifying our positionality, we can begin to identify and examine the assumptions, biases, and values that may guide our thinking, and critically examine our principles, practices, and policies about mental health.

As educators, researchers, and policymakers, we want to make clear our own positionalities and identities. We feel this is critical at the outset of a book like this one where we offer advice about how others should improve schools. Our opinions have been shaped by our experiences as both learners and educators. They are therefore shaped by our context and positions in the world. Explaining who we are also models the kind of honest self-reflection and self-awareness we hope you will bring to your examination of yourself and your school as you rethink everything through a mental health lens.

TOM'S POSITIONALITY

It's critical for me to name and be aware of my positionality or social location in this work, which is shaped by a variety of events, experiences, and social groups. It's the angle from which I view schools and mental health issues in schools. Engaging in this critical reflection and identifying areas in which I have privilege is an opportunity to not only present the awareness that I have of myself and the focus of my work but also critically consider what can be done to establish a climate and culture in schools that addresses the mental health needs of all students.

I am a clinical social worker and a school social worker. I've been in social work practice for 48 years. I've been in a school, in the capacity of student, social worker, counselor, teacher, learner, administrator, for 65 consecutive years. Schools and school year routines and structures are familiar in my lived experience and are an essential part of my identity. My experience in school was challenging. My family faced significant economic and mental health struggles. I was an average student but school felt like a safe haven, a place of belonging. It was in high school that I benefited from a rigorous education and supportive learning environment, a community that was based on service and relationships.

My professional degrees are a master's degree in social work practice and a PhD in clinical social work. I've been a student in a Catholic parochial school through the eighth grade, a Catholic seminary for high school and my first year of college, a Catholic university for my undergraduate degree and MSW, and an independent accredited clinical social work program for my PhD. I've worked in therapeutic day schools and public schools, one of which was a high-achieving high school in which I was the social work department chair for 26 years. I've worked in charter schools and independent schools. The experience of being in schools and with a focus upon mental health has been a through-line.

I am white, cisgendered, male, able-bodied, Christian. In most areas of my identity and social location, I hold significant privilege. I acknowledge the interconnection between the multiple identities that I hold and recognize that as we consider mental health in schools there's a focus upon our individual experiences but also a critical need to consider societal and cultural factors, and to identify the role they play that may be political, economic, and structural. It also provides an opportunity to know that through cultural humility, we recognize the limitations of what we know but remain open to hearing, understanding, and honoring how we perceive the world and the experience of others. Engaging in this exercise helps us to identify privilege, particularly white privilege, and how it shapes our understanding of school climate culture and the needs of all students. I am also a husband, a father, and grandfather, whose hope is that schools are a place where all children can thrive.

TIM'S POSITIONALITY

Like Tom, schools have been my "home" for decades. Growing up in the second half of the 20th century, I thrived in schools, whether traditional K–12 schools, Catholic schools, or in an experimental, "open" classroom school. As a middle-class, white, cisgendered, able-bodied male, I encountered very few obstacles to my success in schools from kindergarten through graduate school. That success is one of the reasons why I chose to enter teaching as a profession. Schools were a place I felt safe, supported, and successful.

My experiences as a teacher, administrator, and teacher–educator are part of the reason for my deep interest in promoting mental health in schools. Over the past 30 years, I have learned from each of the thousands of students I have taught that context and identity are critical elements of anyone's lived experience and their perceptions. Early in my career, I thought I taught "kids" or "classes." Now I realize that I teach individuals. There is no generic lesson plan that works for everyone. And the most important thing I can do as a teacher is to build a relationship with a student so I can provide them with the best experience and support. In doing that, I have had the privilege of helping young people navigate stress, anxiety, trauma, depression, and suicidal ideation, as well as understanding their own race, class, gender, ability, and place in the world. I have also helped teachers, staff, and colleagues navigate their own individual battles with mental health and illness. I've worked with many parents and families on better supporting their children. From them, I have found my voice to lead others to reenvision schools as places where support, safety, and relationships are as important as academic learning.

My other reason for dedicating my life to mental health are my friends and family. I take this work personally because it has been personal. As is true with anyone, I have had my own battles with mental illness, including physical ailments brought on by stress and anxiety. As a very self-reflective individual, I have been hyperaware of my own emotions and the impact they can have on others. More importantly, I have watched the people I love most dearly grapple with mental illness in both small and big ways. It has given me an "insider" view of their struggles and their triumphs as well as the health-care professionals and educators who have been critical to the well-being of my loved ones and me. I want our schools to be locations of belonging, caring, and learning. I believe they can be.

OUR WORK TOGETHER

We have known each other as colleagues for over 30 years. We taught and served in leadership roles at the same high school for much of that time, Tom as a social worker and Social Work Department chair and Tim as an English teacher, department coordinator, and principal. It was during Tim's tenure as principal that we worked in tandem on responding to the many mental health issues facing the students, staff, and community in a large high school. In Tim's first year as principal, we managed the response to the death of two staff members, a murder–suicide involving the family of a current student, and the suicide deaths of a parent and a recent graduate. That year cemented our relationship as colleagues working to improve the health and well-being of those around us in this school. During those years, it was common practice for us to check in with each other weekly to make sure we were each doing OK and to call each other at any time with news of another tragedy or loss in our community.

As it happened, we both left the school at the same time and decided to continue working together on issues related to mental health, social and emotional learning, and school climate. For 10 years, we have crisscrossed the Midwest, working with teachers, administrators, and families on recognizing the signs of suicide; the relationship between the mind, body, and brain; and how to engage in healthy practices and SEL skill-building that can help before, during, and after a crisis. We believe that a healthy school before a crisis can be a healthy school after a crisis, but only if that school and its members engage in a whole-child, whole-person, whole-school approach to mental health and wellness.

CREATING A MENTAL HEALTH ACTION PLAN

We both believe that schools need to reenvision themselves through a mental health lens. In doing so, a school would make different decisions about how to operate on an hourly, weekly, and annual basis. Social and emotional learning would be equal to academic learning. The student's experience from the moment they wake in the morning, through their entire school day, till the time they go to sleep would be seen through this lens of mental health and learning. The classroom would be set up and run differently if mental health was given equal attention as academic success. And with only a few changes, the school itself would begin to feel and act in a way that supported individual needs, relationships, and collective empathy.

This text is our attempt to give teachers, staff, administrators, board members, parents, and community members a blueprint for developing their own Mental Health Action Plan (MHAP) and start enacting it. A complete template of the MHAP is located in the Appendix. Along the way, we will refer to sections of it that you should complete based on your school context. We will also be including "Pause and Reflect" questions within each chapter for you to use on your own or with a school leadership team to think about the issues being presented and how they connect to your overall plan.

YOUR CONTEXT AND POSITIONALITY

A good starting point for developing any MHAP is to explore your own personal identity and context, just as we have done in this chapter. What are your identities? What past experiences have shaped your worldview? What were your experiences like as a learner in schools? What is your opinion of and experience with mental health and mental illness? What strengths can you bring to redesigning your classroom or school? This kind of self-reflection is critical to transparency and honesty as you begin to design your approach.

The next step is to take a long, honest look at your school and community. What are the assets and strengths of your school and community? How can you build upon these? What aspects do you want to make sure remain?

How does organizational history and memory get brought into your MHAP without getting in the way of innovation? What are the nonnegotiables that must be maintained in any design? This is also the moment to think about all the challenges facing your school and community. List them and talk about them. This kind of acknowledgment, again with lots of honesty, can put "all your cards on the table" and prepare you for the design phase that takes them into account. You'll want to look at past surveys, reports, and data, as well as how things are today. Get all your stakeholders to identify both strengths and weaknesses. Ask people outside your school and community to weigh in on their perspectives of your school and your assets and challenges. This kind of "critical friend" perspective is also important.

PAUSE AND REFLECT

Take a moment to think, discuss, or write about these questions:

1. What identities do you hold?

2. How have your overall past experiences shaped who you are today?

3. What is your opinion of and experience with mental health? Mental illness?

4. What are the strengths and challenges of your current school and community context?

OVERVIEW OF THE BOOK AND YOUR PLAN

In the next chapter, we'll spend some time defining mental health and exploring the important "mental models" that undergird our approach to creating mentally healthy schools. We will lay out important facts and considerations when beginning to develop your Mental Health Action Plan. You'll also link your school vision and mission to your approach to mental health.

In Chapters 3, 4, and 5, we will dig into the different levels of mental health and mental illness by using the Multitier System of Support (MTSS) model to organize the implementation of a MHAP. In each of these chapters, we identify the challenges schools face with increasingly more complicated mental health issues. Then we explore the ways some schools have chosen to respond to these issues. Tier 1 is the most important because it addresses the needs of ALL students and adults in a school. It is also the place where we can do the most work in preventative strategies to increase prosocial behaviors, resilience, and positivity. Tiers 2 and 3 focus on response systems for supporting students and staff who are grappling with mental health challenges, both small and large. At some point, every one of us will need some kind of additional support!

In Chapter 6, we provide lots of concrete implementation examples. In many ways, this is the most technical or "nuts-and-bolts" section of the book. While we can't address every subtle nuance in implementing your MHAP, we try to address the most essential elements of classroom and school operations so you can make sure that changes are occurring at both the policy level and the instructional level. We also address the need to change school culture and monitor that culture through comprehensive school climate research.

WHAT COULD THIS LOOK LIKE?

Over the years, we have visited many schools across the country and talked with hundreds of teachers and administrators about rethinking schools through the lens of mental health. There are classrooms and schools that are working very hard on this vision but there are, unfortunately, not enough that have transformed themselves into truly mentally healthy schools. It means we don't have enough examples or models we can visit to inspire others or to get help when they are ready to develop their first MHAP. Throughout this book, we will reference examples of schools, classrooms, and organizations that are on the leading edge of creating the schools we need now. For a moment, here at the beginning, let's take a look at a school that is one example of this kind of mental health-focused school.

One school we have worked with is a large public middle school located in North Carolina. The school culture is a central focus for Anne Marie Adkins, principal, and Jesse DiMartino, dean of culture. Entering into year two, the school has led with restorative practices, while keeping what is best for students at the forefront. Principal Adkins says the vision for the school is simple and impactful: "Our school learning community collaborates to facilitate equitable outcomes and growth through social, emotional, and academic opportunities." Their core values are defined as the following:

- Love of Learning and Perseverance
- Curiosity and Creativity
- Teamwork and Kindness
- Open-Mindedness and Fairness
- Integrity and Self-Control

This vision comes to life in many aspects of the school's intentional systems, structures, and design. The physical space is inviting and allows for collaborative spaces throughout the building so students can fluidly collaborate. The school's systems and structures reverberate what is best for kids as they strive toward an intentionally inclusive strengths based learning environment. It was designed to ensure an inclusive environment that provides opportunities for students to have their voice heard and included in their learning during sixth, seventh, and eighth grades.

For example, before opening the school, the administrators led the staff on an exercise of following a fictitious student through their day... and life! Adkins and DiMartino write, "This helped guide us to design what we wanted students to feel and experience upon arrival, throughout the school day, and then finally through dismissal. As a result, we now have staff positioned all throughout the building and outdoors to positively/warmly greet students each morning and then to send them at the end of the day." Several times each year, school leaders and the dean of culture meet with the staff to review current structures, expectations, experiences, and student feedback to make changes to the school system "to build a runway for students so they can enter a calm, welcoming, and inclusive environment."

Other feedback from students, staff, and families led to other changes in the traditional school day that are focused on mental health. All sixth grade students are enrolled in a course focusing on social and emotional learning. In designing the daily and weekly schedule, administrators built in time in the master schedule on Wednesdays for students and staff to meet together for in-school clubs so no one would be left out. The school also adopted a year-round calendar that is flexible and differentiated based on student needs. Coteaching is also a feature of the classroom so teamwork is modeled by the teachers and multiple adults can support individual students.

School safety and relationships are paramount. The principal and school resource officer (SRO) work collaboratively each day to put the socio-emotional needs of students first so they feel socially, emotionally, and physically safe with all staff, including the SRO. The SRO connects with students in the hallways, cafeteria, and attends classes or engages in lessons alongside them. The Principal and SRO have met with parents proactively to ensure a situation does not escalate into a higher level situation with consequences.

Professional development for teachers and staff is created and delivered in house, focusing on the school's mission and learning about child development, neuroscience, diversity, learning sciences, and instructional practices. Adkins and DiMartino say, "Collecting targeted data is essential in noticing patterns of student behavior and teacher practices. These data points, along with resolution types used, give us the ability to deliver intentional professional development opportunities."

With the creation of systems and structures to mitigate exclusionary practices and strengthen schoolwide tier 1 skills, the administrators and teachers embrace the mindset of being a "Warm Demander," something they learned from the work of Zaretta Hammond (2015). "We know Warm Demanding to be the capacity of educators to be caring adults that value both the student and teacher relationships while holding high expectations for all students," Adkins says. "These expectations are the foundation in which classroom culture is anchored."

With that in mind, they shifted to the language of classroom commitments, which are cocreated via a facilitated process between teachers and students. These are then used as the foundation for all the documents, processes, and programs created throughout the school. Adkins explains, "Our Tiered Discipline Flow Chart is intentionally designed to buffer the school to prison pipeline by requiring Tier 1 behaviors to align with Tier 1 restorative consequences that keep students in their learning environment. We utilize a Support Pass system in which teachers can request support for Tier 2 behaviors as support staff triage and implement the appropriate restorative approach."

The pass is therefore designed to reinforce the skills they want to build within their educators, such as: identifying the appropriate tier of the behavior exhibited, Identifying student emotional state, identifying their own emotional state while engaging with students, taking prior actions before outsourcing the behavior and possibility of transferring the relational status to the support staff.

The school also embraces restorative practices. Restorative practices are a way of strengthening relationships and connections with communities through the use of a series of approaches and tools. Shifting from punitive to restorative discipline is behind the restorative practices mindset. The circle process is the foundational piece of restorative practice. Staff utilize circles weekly in their classrooms, utilizing a variety of methods:

- Check-ins
- Group reflection
- Review of content
- Strengthen relationships
- Refining communication skills
- Develop and showcase character strengths
- Collaboration with peers
- Valuing the opinion of others
- Establish school community

One student describes how the school is different: "I have been a student here for 7th and 8th grade. When I came in 7th grade, one difference I noticed between my last middle school and this middle school was that the students had more opportunities to express ourselves and we could be heard by the staff members better than my old school. At my old school they didn't try to understand where the students were coming from, they just suspended them. At this school we have mediation. Mediation is where two or more students sit together and talk about their issues and solve them."

Adkins and DiMartino believe all this work developing a shared vision and focus among teachers and staff changes the very nature of schooling for everyone: "As we strengthen teacher skill sets on managing student behavior via professional development, we begin to enhance teacher self-efficacy in managing 'challenging' behaviors resulting in increased instructional time and improved relationships, as we aim for the least restrictive learning environment for all."

A CALL TO ACTION

Our schools should reflect our society and community. In many ways, the school should be the center of our community, bringing people together and preparing our children for life in a pluralistic democracy. Schools are also built to provide services that address academic, cognitive, social, emotional, and physical dimensions, but if they only emphasize one of these dimensions, the others may not be addressed as well or at all. We also know that in order for kids to really learn deeply, we must draw from all these dimensions. Traumatized, hungry, or stressed out brains just can't learn, even with the best teachers or curriculum. We must support the whole child if we want to deepen learning.

The schools we need now and into the future must be designed with a whole child perspective. By combining the science of learning with the science of mental health, we can accomplish this goal. It will lead to students who are much more prepared for the challenges of life, whether personal, professional, or societal. It will also result in educators who are better able to do their jobs and stay focused on the kids in front of them. Our schools will become more positive and engaging places that hold the hope for the future for our communities and country. There is no more important responsibility than that.

CREATING YOUR MENTAL HEALTH ACTION PLAN: A TEMPLATE

Take some time to work with your school-based team to think through the following elements of your comprehensive Mental Health Action Plan. The full plan template is located in Appendix A.

School Vision, Mission, Motto

1. Our school's vision is

2. Our school's mission is

3. Our school's motto is

Vision and Mission: Operationalizing Our Core Values and Beliefs

What one sentence represents your school's or district's core values or beliefs about each of the following? Identify at least one specific program, practice, or service that represents your core values or beliefs in that area:

- Children: _____
- Teachers/Staff: _____
- Parents: _____
- Teaching: _____
- Learning: _____
- Assessment: _____
- Behavior: _____
- Mental health: _____
- Physical health: _____
- Equity: _____
- Community: _____
- Relationships: _____

REFERENCES

American Psychological Association. (2022, November 15). *Increased need for mental health care strains capacity*. https://www.apa.org/news/press/releases/2022/11/mental-health-care strains#:~:text=Additionally%2C%20two%2Dthirds%20of%20psychologists,that%20you %20are%20not%20alone

Centers for Disease Control. (2022). *Data and statistics on children's mental health*. https:// www.cdc.gov/childrensmentalhealth/data.html

Hammond, Z. (2015). *Culturally responsive teaching and the brain: Promoting authentic engagement and rigor among culturally and linguistically diverse students*. Corwin.

Mental Health Association. (2021, October 19). *State of mental health in America*. https:// mentalhealthmonmouth.org/2022-state-of-mental-health-in-america/

National Alliance on Mental Illness. (2019). *Mental health in schools*. https://www.nami.org/ Advocacy/Policy-Priorities/Improving-Health/Mental-Health-in-Schools

Sameroff, A. (Ed.). (2009). *The transactional model of development: How children and contexts shape each other*. American Psychological Association.

CHAPTER 2

....

MENTAL HEALTH AND MENTAL MODELS

I am a teacher at heart, and there are moments in the classroom when I can hardly hold the joy. When my students and I discover uncharted territory to explore, when the pathway of a thicket opens up before us, when our experience is illuminated by the lightening-life of the mind-then teaching is the finest work I know.

—Parker Palmer, The Courage to Teach, 2007

Out of necessity and crisis, mental health has become a greater focus in contemporary society broadly and in schools specifically. While this represents a positive change in terms of openness, understanding, and de-stigmatizing mental illness, it has also occurred because of a very real increase in threats and profound challenges to our health and wellness. The COVID-19 Pandemic revealed the mental health crisis in a stark way. The *Journal of the American Medical Association* reported in 2022 on the impact of the pandemic and school closures on children from eleven countries, finding that up to 60% of students experienced strong distress during the pandemic, in particular symptoms of anxiety and depression (Viner et al., 2022). There was an increase in screen time and social media use and a decline in overall physical activity.

Defining how we think about mental health is the first step school leaders must take in developing a strong Mental Health Action Plan (MHAP). One way of thinking about mental health is to focus on the concepts of wellness or well-being. According to the World Health Organization (2022), mental health is more than just the absence of mental illness or a cluster of symptoms as determined by a disease model approach. It is "a state of well-being in which an individual realizes his or her own abilities, can cope with the normal stresses of life, can work productively and is able to make a contribution to his or her community." Embedded in this definition is a person's ability to self-reflect on strengths and challenges. It also points to coping with adversity and resilience in light of stress and normal stressors. Finally, it speaks to a person's ability to be productive and additive to the world around them. All of this would result in a person being "well" or "mentally healthy." It also means that we consider relationships and how the environment and social context can help us to understand and address mental health in our schools.

The definition of *mental health* is complex and encompasses an array of dimensions. If we are going to strive for schools that are healthy and dedicated to supporting the health of students and adults, then it is important to start with a clear working definition of mental health such as the one offered above from the World Health Organization. Clearly, one of the first moves a school or district should make when delving into this work would be to come up with a definition and understanding of mental health that the entire school community can agree upon.

We also believe our beliefs are governed by underlying assumptions and frameworks called "mental models." For example, an American driver traveling to Australia can be disoriented by driving on the left side of the road. Their mental model of how to drive is based on the assumption that you can only drive on the right side of the road. These mental models can help us process new information and tackle challenges but they can also get in the way of seeing new possibilities or changing the way we do things. As an example, many of us maintain the mental model of a classroom as rows of desks facing the front where a teacher should be standing and lecturing. It took a long time for the concept of learning stations to take hold in elementary classrooms or moveable chairs for cooperative learning in secondary and college classrooms. As we will see, mental models about concepts like mental health, mental illness, schools, equity, and even children can be powerful forces that we must critically question and, in some cases, change radically if we are to create the schools we need.

PAUSE AND REFLECT

Take a moment to think, discuss, or write about these questions:

1. What is your school's definition of *mental health*?

2. How open is your school community to talking about mental health?

MENTAL MODEL: A DEVELOPMENTAL MODEL FOR THE WHOLE CHILD

In the early part of the 20th century, schooling was perceived to be all about academics, cognition, facts and figures, reading, writing, and arithmetic. The brain was seen as a muscle that needed to be "worked out" through repetition and mental gymnastics. Other aspects of a student and a student's life were often ignored, either consciously or unconsciously. By the 1920s, educators turned away from this academic model and focused more on the overall developmental needs of young people (Schiro, 2012). Educators such as John Dewey promoted this integrated approach to learning and schooling. Dewey suggested that "Education is not preparation for life; education is life itself" (1916). This shifted the focus of schools and learning to include life skills and dispositions like cooperation. It also suggested that learning is deeply rooted in who we are and the world around us.

This whole-child approach to mental health frames the nature versus nurture debate. It prioritizes caring before cognition, or what some people refer to in the saying, "You have to Maslow before you Bloom." It means understanding students from a developmentally informed perspective and on multiple levels, knowing who they are and what they need. We have had significant new advances in science, particularly interpersonal neurobiology (Siegel & Bryson, 2012). Research reveals that brain development and learning are dependent upon social and emotional factors. According to leading researchers, "Learning indeed depends on how nature is nurtured" (Immordino-Yang et al., 2019). Our daily functioning is impacted by a variety of factors and conditions that affect our physical health, mental health, and learning, underscoring the critical need for a whole-child perspective. When considering development, the nature–nurture discourse is not a debate; it's both.

A holistic approach to mental health takes into account the dynamic and reciprocal nature of relationships, individuals, context, environmental factors, and systems. This kind of ecological perspective puts the child at the center of thinking about your school. It looks at how different systems in a school can impact an individual student and all the many ways that we think about that student. For example, risk factors are characteristics that are associated with a higher likelihood of negative outcomes. Protective factors are characteristics of an individual or community that are associated with positive outcomes and can counter risk factors (SAMHSA, 2023). Schools are dynamic systems and continually change. In considering mental health, the risk and protective factors within a school context are critical to consider, along with day to day routines, the level of stress, stressors, the moments of crisis, or national and global events. All of these factors can affect a student, sometimes in ways we don't see easily.

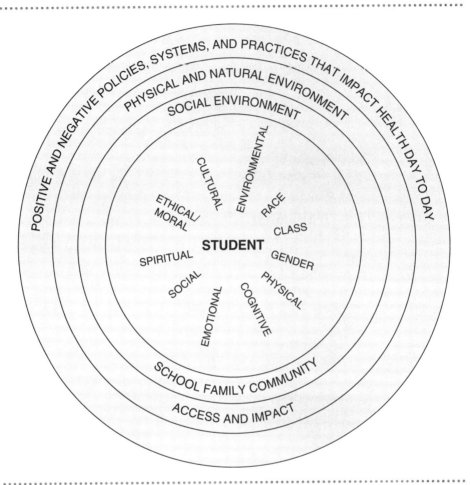

SOURCE: Illustration by Jane Tomlinson.

Think about how well you know your students in terms of these dimensions:

- Physical—How well rested are your students? Are they getting enough sleep? Are their dietary needs being met? Do they understand nutrition? Are they drinking enough water? How much exercise do they get each day? Are their needs being attended to when they are ill or injured?

- Cognitive—How well are they progressing toward developmentally appropriate learning goals? Where do they find joy in their learning? What are their challenges? Are we moving students into the Zone of Proximal Learning or are things too easy or too hard? How do students learn?

- Social—Does the student have positive relationships with other students? Is the student more of an introvert or extrovert? How well does the student pick up on social cues or empathize with others? Is peer pressure impacting your students? Is there a positive relationship with teachers and other adults? What is the level of their social awareness skills? How does the student deal with conflict?

- Emotional—How well do your students regulate their emotions? Can a student talk about their emotions openly with other students and adults? Does a student misunderstand the emotions of others? What is their emotional awareness?

- Spiritual—What role does spirituality play in their lives? Can they articulate a purpose in their life that motivates them? Are there any religious or cultural elements in their lives that can be considered assets to their development? What are their interests and passions?

- Morals/Ethics—How do your students make decisions about themselves and others? Is there an interest in making the world a better place? Of altruism? What forces are shaping their beliefs and values? How do they manage and make difficult decisions?

- Cultural—What are the cultural identities of your students? How do cultural values, customs, events, art, and food, for example, impact their daily lives and shape who they are? How do these cultural experiences align with those of the school?

- Environmental—How does the world around your students impact their lives and development? What are the protective factors and community assets that nurture them? What are the risk factors they are facing? How do things like technology and social media help or hinder their development?

Knowing each student well and knowing their past, present, and future in regard to each of these dimensions is a critical first step in creating a holistic approach to mental health in your school.

Let's pause for a moment and give you a chance to think about the students in your school and the students you have encountered in your life. Think about a healthy student, someone who is meeting that definition of *mental health* from earlier. What are the words you think of when you think of a healthy student? What words would you use to describe that student? Now think about a student you know or have worked with whom has struggled with their health, either physically or mentally. How would you describe that student? What are the words you think of when you think of a student who is distressed and struggling with mental health? Chances are you were able to quickly come up with a list of descriptive words for both students. For healthy students you might have chosen *engaged, connected, well-rested*, or *positive*. For struggling students, the words may have been *absent, aggressive, disconnected*, or *stressed*.

As we work with hundreds of teachers and administrators, we notice that these descriptors are often important indicators of health and wellness, but more importantly they indicate how well educators know their kids. Another activity we have seen schools engage in is to put up the names or, even better, photos of every child in their school. Then they bring in the entire staff—teachers, support staff, custodians, aides, administrators—and ask them to put a sticker or Post-it next to each student they know well, sometimes including a detail to show they really know that student. Next, the entire staff steps back and takes a look at which kids have a lot of connections and which kids have few or none. This activity can identify the students we are clearly supporting well but also kids who need additional support. And when we drill down to look at what details we know about them, then we get a better picture of whether we know the whole child.

We should not take for granted that everyone in the school holds the same values, beliefs, or mental models about children and development. We need clarity. We need to be explicit in our definitions and language surrounding these mental models and ensure we are all talking the same language. Some schools have found great help in developing imagery or graphics that represent their view of the whole child. This may be a place for your school to be explicit about language and to create images about child development, identity, the whole child, community, and belonging. We are also encouraged by the number of schools, districts, and states that are embracing the "Portrait of a Graduate" approach to long-range planning, which has the community imagine the skills, characteristics, and dispositions a student should possess when leaving an elementary, middle school, or high school (Stanford, 2023). This is a truly "whole child" approach to evaluating schools and creating a clear picture of our overall goal.

PAUSE AND REFLECT

Take a moment to think, discuss, or write about these questions:

1. Go back to the list of dimensions for having a whole-child perspective. What role (if any) should a school play in addressing the development of these dimensions?

2. What is the purpose of childhood? What activities should children engage in to grow, learn, and be happy?

3. How do you think and respond to students who learn differently?

MENTAL MODEL: A WHOLE-SCHOOL SYSTEMS THINKING APPROACH

Schools are living systems. Each school has a unique and distinct character. What's the character of your school? As people enter and walk into a school, they can get a "feeling" or sense of what it is like to be here. Just as they take a holistic, whole-child approach to working with students, school leaders must take a "systems thinking" approach to mental health across the school. Like human beings, schools are complex with both independent parts that must function well and multiple systems that must work in concert with each other. The ability of a school leader to keep "the forest and the trees" in mind when making decisions is critical to school leadership, and for creating a mentally healthy culture and climate.

A mentally healthy school should be a safe haven, a secure base for all students, where students not only are safe but feel safe. "What is the emotional health of your school?" is a question that anchors our attention to the mental health of a school. When students feel safe physically and psychologically, when they experience belonging, connection and community, and when learning engages them cognitively, socially, and emotionally, then they can bring their whole selves to school.

A whole-school approach centers the experience of learning for all students but also considers the mental health and social support of its teachers, staff, parents, and community. A holistic approach is an aligned, integrated partnership. Adults in and around the school play a crucial role in this web of relationships and in the proper functioning of the whole school system. As we will see later, school administrators who only focus on the student-related aspects of a school are missing essential partners in building a whole-school approach that can benefit students.

The same mental model we used earlier for the whole child can be applied to the whole-school. Here are some questions to think about when determining the "health" of your school as a whole:

- Physical—Are classrooms well lit, ventilated, and comfortable? Are the public spaces like hallways, bathrooms, and cafeteria clean and well maintained? Do you display artwork, student work, or school spirit messages in the hallways? Are the outdoor school grounds, playgrounds, and facade cared for? How do students get to school? How do they enter the building? How do you manage safety and security? When a visit approaches and enters the building, what do they see and how are they treated?

- Cognitive—How are you creating a "culture of learning" in your school? Is the focus of the school on learning rather than achievement? Is the classroom experience all about the students or all about the teacher? Are academic achievements recognized as much as competitive or athletic achievements? What is your approach to neurodivergent learners and different ways of learning? Do you take a deficit view of learning or a strengths-based view?

- Social—Do people know each other well? How do you promote healthy relationships between students and between staff? With parents? What are the planned events for bringing together the entire community? Is the environment warm, welcoming, and inviting? Do people feel connected and experience belonging?

- Emotional—How are you developing a "culture of caring" in your school? How are positive events celebrated in your community? What venues and processes allow people to raise concerns or process emotions? What are the stressors facing the students, staff, community, and school in general? How do you process crisis situations or loss?

- Spiritual—How are religious holidays and traditions recognized and managed? Is there outreach to local religious organizations in the community? What is the nature of school spirit in the school?

- Moral—Has the school and community identified core values? What matters most in your school? Does the school take part or host discussions about moral and ethical issues? Is there an organized approach or curriculum for character education, civics, or social and emotional learning? Are policies and practices compliance oriented or restorative? Do they align with your values?

- Cultural—Is there a clear understanding of the school's mission and vision? How are new students, staff, and parents oriented to the school's culture? What symbols and slogans represent the school's culture? How is school climate research used as a feedback loop about the culture? What cultural values and practices are privileged, celebrated, or overlooked?

- Environmental—How does the area around the school impact the day to day lives of students, staff, and families? What community organizations and assets can help support the school? How engaged are your students and staff in your community? Is the school seen, used, and valued as a "community center"? What is your school's philosophy on technology, phones, devices, and social media? What local, national, or international issues might impact your students and staff?

In a whole-school approach to mental health, it is critically important to have a deep understanding of what the community and stakeholders in the school *believe* about education and the mission and vision of the school. This includes acknowledging its past, present, and potential future regarding an array of philosophical and ideological stances on things like these:

- The purpose of school and schooling

- The responsibility of the school

- Children and the purpose of childhood

- Definition of *knowledge*

- Learning and the learning sciences

- Research-based teaching practices and pedagogical knowledge

- Role of teachers

- Curriculum and curriculum theory

- Formative and summative assessment

- Social and emotional learning
- Physical development and wellness
- Mental health

It is actually a rare occurrence for students, teachers, administrators, and parents to talk about any of these topics, let alone reach a clear vision and articulated agreement about each of them. The problem with leaving them unspoken is we lose the opportunity to work collectively toward them. So we really need to begin by acknowledging how each of these beliefs is foundational and has a gigantic impact on what happens every day in a school or classroom. We need to be honest about what the school as a whole believes about each one. And then we need to agree on what we want our school to be like in each of those areas. We need to do the work, the difficult and challenging process, of intentionally identifying what things matter in centering mental health.

PAUSE AND REFLECT

Take a moment to think, discuss, or write about these questions:

1. Look at the lists above of dimensions and philosophies of education. Is there clarity among most stakeholders in your school about what our beliefs or goals are in each of those areas? Could you articulate that shared belief for each one?

2. What is your school's mission, vision, and culture regarding mental health?

3. How would you describe your school's culture? What are the explicit examples of that culture? What is more implicit? What is not being asked about school culture?

MENTAL MODEL: A CULTURE OF CARING

In his seminal work *The Courage to Teach*, Parker Palmer (2017) suggested that emotion is central to the work we do as teachers. This quote has positioned us in considering the mental health challenges that are evident in schools and the challenges facing teachers and administrators in the classroom and school environment.

> *Small wonder, then, that teaching tugs at the heart, opens the heart, even breaks the heart—and the more one loves teaching, the more heartbreaking it can be . . . The courage to teach is the courage to keep one's heart open in those very moments when the heart is asked to*

(Continued)

(Continued)

hold more than it is able, so that teacher and students and subject can be woven into the fabric of community that learning, and living, require.

The work we do in schools addressing mental health issues is emotional work. Our experiences can be heartwarming, ones of inspiration and wonder. But they also can deeply touch the vulnerability, fragility, and challenges that are regularly faced in schools today. Any profession that cares for human beings leads to this dichotomy. Somehow, we have to learn how to "hold" both.

Just as doctors, nurses, and social workers have professional codes of conduct and take oaths to ensure patients are cared for, education systems should reflect this same value and be seen at every level and within every interaction we have with those who inhabit the school. We call this mental model a "Culture of Caring."

When thinking about culture, we consider beliefs, values, patterns of relationships, language, practices, and routines. Each provides us with a sense of identity, meaning, and a framework for what it is like to belong. What we are talking about here is knowing your school culture really, really well. It means understanding who you are and what you believe collectively. School culture is the force that pulls together all the disparate parts of a school into a collective whole. It is often defined as "the way we do things around here," or the written and unwritten "rules" for an organization.

School culture can be seen in the Student Handbook, the teacher's contract, and the school board minutes. It is the feeling a visitor gets when walking into a building or through the halls. It is the school mascot and colors and song, as well as the ceremonies and events we put on every week and every year. It is how a new student is treated in the cafeteria or the playground or the classroom. School culture can be either positive or negative (or neutral!), but it is always there, embedded in everything we do. The goal, of course, is to create a positive school culture academically, socially, emotionally, and physically for all kids and adults who interact with the school. In this way, school culture focuses and frames the school community.

We know about culture by staying attuned to the school's climate. School climate is an indicator of school culture and how systems are operating in a school generally. When done well, school climate research can also serve as a valuable evaluation tool on mental health and change efforts. Some states and districts now require administrators to collect school climate data from students, staff, and parents via survey and focus group interviews. There are several very good school climate surveys available or a school can create their own. The National School Climate Center is a great resource for getting started in school climate research. School leaders should collect climate data every one or two years and then analyze that data for ways of improving school culture. We suggest doing both school climate surveys and focus group or individual interviews, in addition to analyzing data that is already collected each year such as demographics, testing, attendance, and behavior issues.

Culture and context go hand in hand. A culture of genuine care and compassion is one that is attuned to the mental health of its students. Culture is about connection, identity, belonging and care. Appreciating that teaching is emotional work, that learning takes place within significant relationships, and in a community that supports young people can result in a true culture of care (Comer, 1995). But as with any important endeavor, this culture must be cultivated and attended to on a daily basis. It is how students are treated as they enter the building, walk the halls, or enter a classroom. It is every student knowing there is at least one adult (or many) they can turn to if they have a question or a problem. It is the engagement in learning in every lesson, every day. It is how we greet each other in the hallway, speak to parents on the phone, or the words we use in the weekly email home. Teachers and leaders cultivate this culture every single day!

PAUSE AND REFLECT

Take a moment to think, discuss, or write about these questions:

1. Is "caring" a core value in your work as an educator?

2. Is "caring" a core value in your school?

3. What challenges do you face in aligning those values with your practice? What do you do when your values conflict with each other?

4. What evidence exists that shows you or your school cares for students? Staff? Families?

MENTAL MODEL: A CONTINUUM OF CARE

The application and evidence of a culture of caring can be seen by how schools utilize a "continuum of care." A continuum of care is an organized, integrated, and aligned set of practices, policies, and strategies that considers the needs, issues and resources of the individuals and the school community. It encompasses all the ways, both big and small, that a system cares for its constituents. The concept was developed in the 1980s and 1990s by health care professionals and the U.S. Department of Housing and Urban Development (HUD) to address homelessness, utilizing the framework of a continuum of care as a concept of integrating a comprehensive range of services covering all levels of intensity (Blasco, 2017; Evashwick, 1989, 2005). It is a wonderful example of "systems thinking," where we simultaneously consider both the individual and the larger ecosystem around that individual.

Applying this concept in schools starts with a needs assessment of risks, resources, and protective factors. A well-defined and executed continuum of care considers every way we support a student or staff member or parent as well as connections and partnerships with and within the community. It is process-oriented, structured, and relational, and it looks at individual and collective needs. Next, the continuum of care must develop an environment where that child, with all their individual needs, will be able to flourish, grow, and learn; where they are seen, respected, and engaged. A well-designed and well-run continuum of care allows all students to thrive academically, socially, emotionally, and physically, creating conditions and opportunities to optimally and equitably utilize internal resources and programs, as well as external resources and support.

Components of a continuum of care are likely already in place in most schools. The first is a staff of educators who care and an overall culture of caring. The second is a multitiered system of support (MTSS) that considers the needs of all students and of individuals. We'll talk more about MTSS in a later section but for now this means the structures in place to support a range of students and to differentiate teaching and assessments for every child. The third is to focus on curriculum and resources that each student feels connected to and engaged with. Finally, there must be alignment of all systems, tools, people, and resources. Schools with advisories, student services teams, professional learning communities, and all-school wellness teams are already creating systems that can be integrated and aligned.

A comprehensive continuum of care considers a wide range of strategies, structures, and tools. The components would address prevention, early intervention, intervention, crisis response, at-risk students, transitional needs, and high-risk or vulnerable students. This kind of whole-school mental health approach builds structures and systems that are comprehensive, coordinated, integrated, and aligned. It looks closely at needs, resources, and access to those resources, as well as barriers.

PAUSE AND REFLECT

Take a moment to think, discuss, or write about these questions:

1. What systems and processes does your school have in place that would constitute a continuum of care?

2. Where are there gaps in your continuum of care?

3. What barriers might exist to creating a continuum of care?

4. What would need to change to ensure each student experienced complete caring throughout their day and life in your school?

MENTAL MODEL: THINKING DIFFERENTLY ABOUT MENTAL HEALTH

Schools are long-standing institutions and have changed only slightly over the past 100 years. That means their approach to mental health or mental illness can often be mired in traditional approaches and thinking that are well behind what we need today. We also have a long history of how mental illness has been viewed and addressed in American society and need to recognize the stigma, challenge, and impact of the broader culture on our thinking about mental health. Establishing a mental model that thinks outside of those traditional approaches and embraces creativity, innovation, and change over tradition is critical and requires a certain level of bravery as we challenge outdated perceptions and processes.

Many of the skills and practices that we may need to develop to take a mental health approach to education require thinking about the kind of support schools offer to individual students, families, teachers, and community members—a broader audience than schools have traditionally focused upon. Schools may also need to focus more upon social and emotional learning, as well as addressing the physical well-being of individuals. Schools need to consider all we've learned from the science of stress, including the research on developmental implications of stress upon children, the stress response and the body, brain and mind, toxic stress, and the cumulative effects of trauma and adversity on both the well-being of students as well as adults.

Alarming indicators of risks that relate to mental health, including school shootings, racism, and increased levels of depression and anxiety, all challenge us to embed practices, policies, and innovative programs that address mental health into schools. We are in a critical moment of time when mental health needs a holistic approach and mental models that integrate the art and science of social and emotional learning from a whole child, school and community perspective. We need models that consider development, trauma informed care, and systems that integrate MTSS as a continuum of care and compassion.

For too long, schools have been islands unto themselves, trying valiantly to solve multiple problems facing kids and parents. However, schools can't take on these challenges alone. They must reach out to other organizations in the community to create new ways of working together and to develop partnerships. An example of this kind of outside the box, systemic thinking would be an All-School Wellness Team, where stakeholders would come together to address the wellness of all students, staff, and schools in the community. In schools with these kinds of teams, all members of the community have a "voice" and a "seat at the table" to help solve problems.

These ideas are not new nor are they impossible; many schools across the country have tried these with great success. Unfortunately, there are still so many places where it is difficult to even conceptualize a different way to "do school." If we are going to create a comprehensive mental health action plan that puts mental health front and center in everything we do, then educators, school leaders, and community members need to take on a new mental model that embraces "thinking outside of the box" and leans into innovation and creativity.

MENTAL MODEL: A MULTITIERED SYSTEMS OF SUPPORT APPROACH TO MENTAL HEALTH

Multitiered Systems of Support (MTSS) was developed out of concerns for students struggling with academic and behavioral challenges and provided a framework of interventions to address those challenges. Other intervention-based frameworks like Response to intervention (RTI) and Positive Behavioral Interventions and Supports (PBIS) grew out of the Individuals with Disabilities Act (IDEA). The programs, originally designed to address and improve outcomes for students with identified needs and specific education services, can be used and applied to address the experience of ALL students . . . and to mental health!

FIGURE 2.2 AN MTSS APPROACH TO MENTAL HEALTH (CENTERS FOR DISEASE CONTROL, 2023)

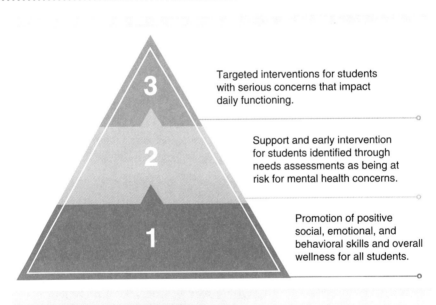

3 — Targeted interventions for students with serious concerns that impact daily functioning.

2 — Support and early intervention for students identified through needs assessments as being at risk for mental health concerns.

1 — Promotion of positive social, emotional, and behavioral skills and overall wellness for all students.

FOUNDATIONAL ELEMENTS

o Professional development and support for a healthy school workforce.

o Family-school-community partnerships.

SOURCE: CDC; Use of the material does not constitute its endorsement or recommendation by the U.S. Government, Department of Health and Human Services, or Centers for Disease Control and Prevention; Material is available on https://www.cdc.gov/

When MTSS is applied from a mental health perspective, it can result in a comprehensive approach that begins with a focus upon what is done for all students. In Tier 1, the continuum of care begins with prevention and early interventions throughout the academic, social, emotional, and physical dimensions of schooling. Tier 1 cultivates awareness and develops knowledge, skills, and strategies about the mind and body and integrates SEL skills in the classroom and culture. It is designed to access, individually and collectively, integrated programs and strategies for all students, staff, and community members. In a sense, everything we do in school for all students can be seen as a Tier 1 strategy. Here, we firmly believe that the most beneficial form of interventions are prevention activities and programs.

We all encounter vulnerability, excessive stress, loss, and traumatic events. At some point every person will need extra support beyond Tier 1, which is where Tier 2 comes in. When the foundational Tier 1 support isn't enough, the school can provide temporary "in the moment" support for students and staff, with the hope that they will return to the foundational Tier 1 support. It's important to note that if the school has built excellent Tier 1 supports then the number of people needing Tier 2 support should be relatively small, maybe 15% to 20% of students and staff at any given time. Every person experiences moments of stress, anxiety, and trauma at some point in their lives, for example, when students are transitioning into or out of a school we often see elevated levels of anxiety. Academically, there are moments when a student might need additional help, especially when grappling with a new or challenging concept. During these moments, schools can implement an array of interventions such as academic support centers, specialized classes, affinity groups, individual counseling, or peer support.

Tier 3 mental health support starts with the foundation of Tiers 1 and 2 to create a highly-individualized and specialized support system for the most vulnerable, at-risk members of the school community. We will always have students and adults in a school who will need this kind of serious support. The hope is that with a strong implementation of Tiers 1 and 2 we can reduce the number of individuals needing Tier 3 support to 5% to 10% of our school population. Thanks to a deeper, more sophisticated understanding of toxic stress, childhood trauma, and mental illness, for example, we can create much better ways to support individuals grappling with the most difficult mental health issues: crisis response, individualized counseling, group counseling, individualized education plans, family and parent support groups, and programs that help students return from hospitalizations. In Tier 3, these targeted interventions are supportive of students who are most vulnerable, often in need of specialized, professional support but with an integrated and coordinated engagement of parents and community partnerships.

In the next few chapters, we will walk through the three tiers of this MTSS approach to mental health, taking a closer look at the challenges facing schools at each level and highlighting potential interventions that can be built into your own Mental Health Action Plan.

Take a moment to think, discuss, or write about these questions:

1. What support systems for students do you have in place? For staff?

2. What is the status of your current approach to MTSS?

3. What structures are in place for supporting students who experience challenges or crisis situations?

CONCLUSION: MENTAL MODELS AS THE FOUNDATION OF YOUR ACTION PLAN

Sweeping changes in our world brought on by technology, social movements, and a global pandemic have resulted in a mental health crisis that is impacting both young and old. We also have a more scientific and deep understanding of brain development, the impact of childhood trauma, and how stress and anxiety can change our minds and bodies. And that same, science tells us that attending to our mental health and physical wellness can build resilience and lead to a happier, healthier life.

Mental health exists on a spectrum: Our schools must not only understand this spectrum, but also must take the lead in integrating mental health into everything they do. They need to consider the myriad of healthy coping strategies, risk and protective factors, and challenges that underlie mental health. They must partner with other schools and community organizations to build a continuum of care so the most vulnerable members of our society can be supported every moment of every day.

In this chapter, we presented some ideas that should be at the center of your development of a Mental Health Action Plan for your school or district. We start with some mental models that can guide your thinking and practice to address mental health and create a common vision and language for practice, skills, and implementation of that plan. This includes a developmentally informed, whole-child, whole-school perspective, which takes an ecological systems perspective to understand children, context, and environmental risk and protective factors. It embeds all this in a continuum of care and uses an MTSS approach to understand and support positive mental health.

We challenge school leaders to think deeply about the questions posed in this chapter about values, beliefs, vision, and mission. They should gather all stakeholders together and spend time digging into these questions and create a kind of "This We Believe" document that reimagines school through the lens of mental health. This document can be the fertile ground needed to grow new systems for academic learning, assessment, after school activities, school building design, professional learning, community, and partnerships, for example.

This reimagined school, powered by these mental models, is possible today because of what schools have always done well: provide a safe place where human beings can grow individually by interacting collectively. The great James Comer (1995) said, "No significant learning can occur without a significant relationship." Schools are the most important learning organizations in the world and have the capacity to leverage the power of relationships to grow young people who are academically, socially, emotionally, and physically strong. To borrow a phrase from Bettina Love (2019), we want more from our children than to just survive; we want them to thrive. Now is the time to reimagine your school so it can attain its potential as a model of wellness.

CREATING YOUR MENTAL HEALTH ACTION PLAN

Take some time to work with your school-based team to think through the following elements of your comprehensive Mental Health Action Plan. The full plan template is located in Appendix A.

Current Context: Data and Needs

1. What is the story of our school?

2. Who are we? What are our needs?

Community Context

1. Demographics (total population, age, race, ethnicity, gender, economic, etc.)

2. Describe your local community context.

3. Protective factors (characteristics of your school and community that are positive)

4. Assets (current resources that support students, staff, and families)

5. Risk factors (characteristics of the school or community that may have a negative impact on students, staff, or families)

```
[                                                                    ]
```

6. Challenges (specific forces, situations, or barriers that have a negative impact on our school)

```
[                                                                    ]
```

7. What do we consider to be the biggest, most critical mental health or socio/emotional need in our school? What does our school need the most help with to improve our mental health? What's missing?

```
[                                                                    ]
```

Existing School Structures

1. How are we organized?

```
[                                                                    ]
```

2. What structures do we rely on to accomplish our mission?

```
[                                                                    ]
```

3. What processes drive our organization or hold us back?

```
[                                                                    ]
```

4. What are our policies and practices as stated in print? How do they address mental health? What's missing? Unclear? Inconsistent?

```
[                                                                    ]
```

5. Is mental health a part of our overall wellness strategy? Where do we explicitly and intentionally address mental health and wellness? Do we have an All-School Wellness team?

Prevention and Intervention
MTSS/RtI: An Integrated Approach With a Continuum of Care

1. How have we structured our school around academics, behavior, mental health?

2. What is our "continuum of care"?

3. In what ways are we "trauma informed"?

REFERENCES

Blasco, A. (2017). *Continuum of care planning*. National Low Income Housing Coalition. https://nlihc.org/sites/default/files/AG-2017/2017AG_Ch07-S06_Continuum-of-Care-Planning.pdf

Centers for Disease Control. (2023). Promoting mental health and well-being in schools. https://www.cdc.gov/healthyyouth/mental-health-action-guide/index.html

Comer, J. (1995). *Lecture given at Education Service Center. Region IV*, Houston, TX.

Dewey, J. (1916). *Democracy and education*. McMillan.

Evashwick, C. (1989). Creating the continuum of care. *Health Matrix*, 7(1), 30–39. PMID: 10293297.

Evashwick, C. (2005). *The continuum of long-term care* (3rd ed.). Thomson Delmar Learning.

Immordino-Yang, M., Darling-Hammond, L., & Krone, C. (2019). Nurturing nature: How brain development is inherently social and emotional, and what this means for education. *Educational Psychologist*, 54(3), 185–204.

Love, B. L. (2019). *We want to do more than survive: Abolitionist teaching and the pursuit of educational freedom*. Beacon Press.

Palmer, P. J. (2017). *The courage to teach* (20th ed.). Jossey-Bass.

Schiro, M. (2012). *Curriculum theory: Conflicting visions and enduring concerns* (2nd ed.). SAGE.

Siegel, D. J., & Bryson, T. P. (2012). *The whole-brain child*. Random House.

Stanford, L. (2023). More states are creating a "portrait of a graduate." Here's why. *Education Week*. https://www.edweek.org/policy-politics/more-states-are-creating-a-portrait-of-a-graduate-heres-why/2023/12

Substance Abuse and Mental Health Services Administration (SAMHSA). (2023). U.S. Department of Health and Human Services. https://www.samhsa.gov/sites/default/files/20190718-samhsa-risk-protective-factors.pdf

Viner, R., Russell, S., Saulle, R., Croker, H., Stansfield, C., Packer, J., Nicholls, D., Goddings, A.-L., Bonell, C., Hudson, L., Hope, S., Ward, J., Schwalbe, N., Morgan, A., & Minozzi, S. (2022). School closures during social lockdown and mental health, health behaviors, and well-being among children and adolescents during the first COVID-19 wave: A systematic review. *JAMA Pediatrics, 176*(4), 400–409. https://doi.org/10.1001/jamapediatrics.2021.5840

World Health Organization. (2022). *Health and well-being*. The Global Health Observatory. https://www.who.int/data/gho/data/major-themes/health-and-well-being

CHAPTER 3

....

TIER 1 MENTAL HEALTH: UNIVERSAL SUPPORTS FOR ALL

An ounce of prevention is worth a pound of cure.

—Benjamin Franklin

Too often, the books, speakers, and workshops on mental health are focused on *responding* to crises. While it is absolutely important to have a well-defined crisis response plan, we feel it is fundamentally more essential to spend time and resources on *prevention*. As the quote that opens this chapter suggests, we can save ourselves confusion and a lot of grief later on by addressing the conditions that lead to greater mental health challenges by better preparing ourselves for those inevitable times when we will face some sort of crisis. The nature of crisis in schools is that it is not a question of "if" a crisis will occur, but "when." That means schools need to build capacities that may prevent as many problems as possible and have strategies and plans ready to address them when they occur.

It is also important to note at this moment that there is no "one-size-fits-all" model for supporting mental health, nor is there a single "silver bullet" that can solve all our problems. As we have noted before, a holistic, systems-thinking approach requires complex and nuanced solutions to our mental health challenges. Whatever we design, whatever our school Mental Health Action Plan looks like, we need to always be mindful of the context and environment we find ourselves in; the resources available; and the students, staff, and families in our own community. That way our plan will be not only comprehensive but relevant to our most important stakeholders.

There is a compelling body of recent research that points to the need to redesign schools with this more comprehensive, cohesive, systems-thinking approach that integrates the academic with social, emotional, and physical concerns. Much of that research can be found in the "Design Principles for Schools" published by the Learning Policy Institute and Turnaround Schools. This important 2021 report, grounded in the science of learning and our deepening understanding of human development, brain research, and wellness, has some of the leading scientists in the world mapping out ways to incorporate all of this knowledge into classroom practice and school systems. It is a call to redesign schools from the ground up, taking into account all the latest and best research. This kind of systems-thinking is essential in today's schools and must include mental health.

In the previous chapter, we introduced multiple mental models that should infuse the redesign of schools through a mental health lens. One of those was the model used for decades in schools for academic and behavior interventions called Multitiered Systems of Support(MTSS) or Response to Intervention(RtI). Because of its widespread use in thousands of schools, the MTSS pyramid is a wonderful mental model for understanding the kinds of mental health support needed in a comprehensive Mental Health Action Plan. And as a true systems approach to thinking, it addresses universal interventions (Tier 1) as well as individualized interventions (Tiers 2 and 3).

In this chapter, we will delve into challenges and interventions of Tier 1, which impacts every student and staff member. It is the basis for all prevention work. It assumes that everyone will have need for some kind of support all the time. It creates the conditions for equitable response and resources. These are the *universal* interventions that are integrated into the school's culture and provide what all students and staff need every day in regards to the academic, physical, social, and emotional dimensions of schooling.

TIER 1: WHAT DO WE MEAN BY "UNIVERSAL"?

Schools are a microcosm of the community. Each member of that community has needs and deserves adequate support, resources, and interventions. A holistic approach to mental health takes into account the person and the environment. It establishes a baseline for success in learning and how we treat each other. Context always matters. Risk and protective factors in the environment must be considered along with the impact of crisis, stress and trauma that each individual and the community will inevitably experience. What are the fundamental needs of every student? What are the basic resources our school will provide to every student? What interventions are available to support every student?

A whole-child, whole-school, whole-community approach sets the stage for universal systems of support. It puts students and staff at the center of everything we do and acknowledges the central role schools play in our lives. It embeds social and emotional learning into the academic classroom. It creates a sense of interdependence, that we're all connected, and that we all belong to something bigger than ourselves. A whole school approach creates an environment where school is a safe haven, a place of connection and belonging, a place of community where people know each other and understand how to be present with each other. It cultivates a readiness to engage in learning but also of care and compassion. Universal support means a community in which everyone has an experience of being cared for.

A universal Tier 1 approach assumes that everything done in a school affects mental health. It creates an infrastructure that is comprehensive, coordinated, integrated and aligned with this question: "How well you know your students?" Mental health must be understood for its depth, complexity, and integration into all aspects of the school. It needs to be considered individually and collectively by all. It recognizes that people move both in and out of mental health throughout their life experiences. Students, staff, and teachers should be explicitly taught about stress, anxiety, and trauma, as well as what we know about the brain. They should also learn and practice mental hygiene such as focused breathing, brain breaks, building relationships, taking a walk in nature, gratitude, and altruism. It takes into account restorative and trauma-sensitive practices and integrates them in and throughout the school's culture. Mental health itself needs to be embedded in the DNA and culture of the school and classroom.

TIER 1 AS PREVENTION AND EARLY INTERVENTION

Because it is universal, Tier 1 mental health support is an essential part of any prevention strategy. Often, prevention strategies are overlooked as we tend to focus on reactive strategies or crisis management. But if we can reduce the need for interventions, we not only save valuable time and money, but we also can create a more positive learning environment. A healthy, safe school culture is essential to the prevention of many mental health challenges. It can also serve as an early warning system for those challenges as an early intervention strategy.

One of the most effective approaches to prevention is awareness and education. A prevention model identifies and evaluates conditions, explores resources, provides solutions to preventable problems, and embeds social and emotional learning into every aspect of a school. Prevention requires the awareness and understanding of mental health, risk factors, and protective factors.

Prevention strategies should embed attitudes, beliefs, and behaviors that both prevent problems like bullying, harassment, and violence, and promote skill-building capacities through teaching and training these skills, including conflict mediation, problem-solving, social and emotional learning, relationship-building, and physical wellness. Consider the resources and strengths that you already have in your school. One often underutilized resource is your students. Providing students with opportunities to learn and utilize SEL skills to address needs and support each other will enrich the climate and culture of the school. Examples may include developing programs like Peer Helping and Peer Mentoring that are designed to promote positive peer relationships, teach problem solving skills and promote healthy relationships. Students tutoring each other or younger students combine academics with SEL skills and relationship-building.

Prevention focuses on creating a climate that encourages mental health and builds community by improving and addressing the conditions that contribute to risk behavior and poor health while building upon strengths and developing resilience. Schools should consider developing a "Prevention Tool Kit" that includes research-based information about stress health, mental health, and brain development; provides opportunities to learn skills and strategies to make responsible decisions and responsible choices; and how to build healthy relationships that are a buffer to life's challenges. It should also provide access to resources that not only offer support but actively engage young people in critical thinking to make informed decisions.

A prevention plan is well integrated and includes strategies that create healthy relationships and an environment that reduces risk and increases capacities. It also includes a focus upon developing secondary and tertiary prevention supports, which we will explore later in Tiers 2 and 3. These address any risk behaviors that have been identified in and around the school and can range from managing stress to more severe issues of drug and alcohol use, mental illness, or suicidal ideation.

An orientation toward prevention focuses on trying to prevent problems before they occur. A universal whole-child, whole-school, whole-community approach, that is integrated, coordinated, communicated, reflective and not reactive, creates a better quality of life in a school and addresses underlying causes that may contribute to risk by identifying risk factors. It attempts to prevent problems, providing resources and tools that equip students and adults in the school and community to help. By focusing on prevention, we address the challenges facing everyone in the school and create pathways for more easily finding success and health.

PAUSE AND REFLECT

Take a moment to think, discuss, or write about these questions:

1. How oriented is your school toward a *universal* approach to support and problem-solving?

2. How much of your school's energy is focused on prevention? (vs. intervention or crisis response) What problems might be solved with a greater focus on prevention?

3. Consider checking out resources such as the CDC Violence Prevention website or the Substance Abuse and Mental Health Services Administration (SAMHSA) toolkit.

4. How do you integrate and align restorative and trauma-sensitive practices in each of the MTSS tiers?

UNIVERSAL CHALLENGES TO EVERYONE

Let's take some time now to identify some of the most common universal challenges about mental health that face students, staff, and schools. If the first step in prevention is awareness then we should be aware of these challenges and understand them well enough to devise Tier 1 strategies to prevent or intervene. These challenges include safety, stigmas, identity, community, equity, environment, and technology. Some of these may seem basic but remember that we want to create universal strategies that would support every individual as well as the collective whole.

SAFETY FIRST: "MASLOW BEFORE YOU BLOOM"

The stress response is encoded in our evolutionary DNA. It's the mind-body-brain connection. It draws and focuses our attention on basic needs, and the most basic instinctual need is survival, both physical, social, and psychological. In 1943, Abraham Maslow identified a hierarchy of needs that impacts motivation and behavior. The hierarchy includes physiological needs, safety needs, love and belonging, esteem, and self-actualization. Some of those basic needs should be addressed in some way before addressing more advanced concepts, like self-actualization. In more recent research on the brain and the stress response, it is clear that some of those basic human needs like safety must be addressed before students can access the cognitive decision-making parts of the brain, things like comprehension or critical thinking that Benjamin Bloom described in his famous taxonomy of thinking. In 2020, as the world was in the throes of the COVID-19 pandemic, this need to first address safety before cognition was made abundantly clear, hence the phrase, "You have to Maslow before you Bloom."

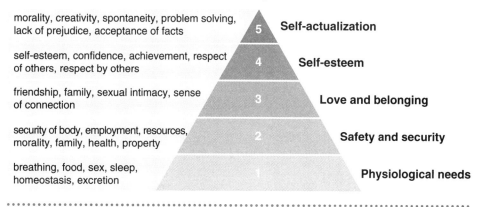

Maslow's hierarchy of needs

morality, creativity, spontaneity, problem solving, lack of prejudice, acceptance of facts	5	**Self-actualization**
self-esteem, confidence, achievement, respect of others, respect by others	4	**Self-esteem**
friendship, family, sexual intimacy, sense of connection	3	**Love and belonging**
security of body, employment, resources, morality, family, health, property	2	**Safety and security**
breathing, food, sex, sleep, homeostasis, excretion	1	**Physiological needs**

SOURCE: Istock.com/PytyCzech

One of the first challenges of building a strong level of Tier 1 in a mentally healthy school is attending to the basic human needs described by Maslow, which is physical safety. A simple way to describe this is "food, clothing, and shelter" but it involves other important elements as well. Clearly, human beings need air, water, and food to live and survive. Unfortunately, too many of our children come to school hungry or malnourished. Clean air is a challenge in some communities and schools. Many of our schools have outdated physical plants that are not well ventilated or introduce iron and other deposits into drinking water. Over 1.1 million students are identified each year as homeless, according to the U.S. Department of Education. This means daily challenges to where a student will live or sleep or the clothing they will wear. It is quite easy for any of these or, worse, several of them to interfere with a student's ability to make sense of math or a poem or world history.

The other important basic physiological need we all have is relationships, something we have mentioned before. Being in a protective relationship with a family member, parent, friend, or trusted adult is powerful when it comes to safety. We also know that a "culture of caring," one of those mental models we wrote about in chapter 2, allows us to build resiliency before, during, and after a stressful time or a crisis. Social connection is a part of human existence and plays a critical role in our feelings of safety and our physical health (Cohen et al., 1997). Once again, the recent global pandemic, in which we all experienced massive social isolation, led to a rise in mental illness and concerns about mental health (Hwang et al., 2020). When it comes to safety, it could be easy to over-look the role relationships have on our feelings and experiences.

We must also consider the differences between physical safety and psycho-logical safety, which for us is encapsulated in the phrase "being safe and feeling safe." Physical safety can be seen in typical school data like detentions, suspensions, and expulsions, or number of physical altercations per year. It can also be in the form of security staff, school resource officers, building security, and camera systems, as well as student behavior in hallways and cafeterias. Psychological safety is determined by feelings, experiences, and relationships. It builds upon trust and respect and integrates listening, con-nections, and the Continuum of Care. It is the notion of a "Beloved Com-munity" suggested by Martin Luther King Jr. where the presence of someone you know helps you feel safe and reduces stress levels, underscoring that relational connections are one of the most powerful ways to buffer stress. These are the foundations for a mentally healthy school: connection, belonging, students who are seen and heard and known.

There are many things a school can due to improve safety, both real and perceived. Ask yourself these questions: Is the environment safe and secure for all students? Have you communicated and practiced your emergency response plan? What are the challenges to food, clothing, and shelter that any of your students are facing? Many schools are embracing a "Community Schools" model that includes a food pantry, basic health support, and free and reduced lunch programs. Schools can also open their doors earlier and stay open later to provide safe spaces for kids and to help families and parents who need to get to their jobs. Schools can also engage students, staff, and parents in training and educational programming related to bullying, harassment, equity, microaggressions, discrimination, stress management, mental health, and social and emotional skills.

Consider the climate of the school. What is the emotional tone? Do students and staff feel safe? Do they have the necessary relational skills and knowledge to cope with stress and some of the day-to-day challenges that schools regularly face? Are there clear policies and procedures that address behavior but more significantly try to get at some of the underlying causes that contribute to health and mental health? What are the challenges that interface and interfere with the day-to-day emotional experiences? Answers to these kinds of questions can be easily collected through school climate surveys, focus groups, and interviews. Every school should have systems for regularly collecting this kind of feedback, either annually or biannually, and how to integrate the findings into real policy decisions and school improvement plans.

Being intentional and explicit in your safety plans could range from activities as simple as a positive climate campaign, emphasizing restorative practices and classroom management as opposed to traditional disciplinary approaches, and employing peer and staff mentoring and coaching. Cultivating psychological safety throughout the school means looking inside and outside the classroom to create an overall environment that can attend to issues of health and safety prevention, as well as early intervention.

PAUSE AND REFLECT

Take a moment to think, discuss, or write about these questions:

1. What does your school due to provide for basic needs such as food, clothing, and shelter? What do your students and families need in your community? How could the school help?

2. Do all of your students feel physically safe at school? Psychologically safe? What about your staff? Visitors to the school?

3. Is your school seen as a "community school" by students, staff, families, and neighbors? What steps could you take to move toward a more community school model?

STIGMA AND STEREOTYPES

It is critical to develop skills, strategies, and practices to cultivate mental health. To be effective in addressing mental health issues in school settings, we must also examine our values, beliefs, and biases. One place to start is examining our own perceptions and stigmas about mental health and mental illness. What are your beliefs about mental health and mental illness? What stereotypes do you have? What is your understanding of the history of mental illness and the expressions of stigma discrimination of students with disabilities? What's the everyday experience of students in your community? What types of programs and practices build awareness about mental illness? Do all of your students have access to mental health resources? Do you take into account culturally sensitive beliefs about mental health? In order to combat stigma around mental health, we must normalize conversations about mental health and talk about stress, anxiety, and trauma in the same way we talk about allergies or public transportation.

Schools and educators can help combat stigmas and stereotypes about mental health by incorporating it into the curriculum, offering parent workshops about stress, anxiety, and trauma, and by providing resources on school websites. Do your written policies and procedures support wellness and mental health for students and staff? Several school districts we work with provide daytime and evening parent workshops on these kinds of topics. Principals lead book group discussions on a monthly book related to parenting or child development. Guest speakers are brought into the school to work with students about mental health. School counselors lead small groups on topics like loss, depression, or substance abuse. Staff meetings should also focus on these topics, not only regarding the mental health of students, but also adult mental health topics. The more we talk about these issues and the more science-based material we provide, the greater the chance we will have the right words and vocabulary to use in discussing mental health with students, colleagues, and families.

DISCONNECTION FROM RELATIONSHIPS AND COMMUNITY

Early in the COVID-19 pandemic, we found ourselves socially isolated in a way most people had never experienced. Fear, both real and perceived, forced us to shelter in place in our homes and away from large gatherings that would have normally provided us with connection and community. This was a period of heightened stress, anxiety, isolation, and loneliness. There are many other forces that keep us disconnected from each other including technology, remote work, economic or racial segregation, or school closings. In schools, there are too many examples of isolating students from each other through grade levels, ability grouping and tracking, and multiple campuses. Even in a classroom, students can be isolated from each other if all the instruction is teacher centered and students don't get a chance to collaborate or engage with each other. Yet childhood and adolescence are essential moments for learning how to get along with others and for leveraging connection to support resilience and coping skill development. A culture of caring and a sense of belonging are key to combating separation and isolation (Hwang et al., 2020).

Schools can and should be places of connection and community. This starts with outreach to families so students and their family members feel welcome and connected to the school. Weekly emails and messages from the teacher and principal to families are easy ways to create this connection and maintain communication. Some schools create parent/family "offices" in the building where parents can come to access a computer or meet with a staff member. The next place where community can be developed is the classroom. Teachers have a tremendous opportunity to create classroom environments where kids connect with each other and where collaboration is common. These classrooms put students at the center of activity and are not places where teachers lecture day after day. Instead, students engage in both individual and group learning tasks like project-based learning or inquiry projects. Schools can also provide clubs, activities, performing arts, visual arts, and athletics to give students yet another way to connect with each other and build community. For some students, their reason for coming to school might be one of these extracurricular activities!

PAUSE AND REFLECT

Take a moment to think, discuss, or write about these questions:

1. Are there topics in your school and community that people are nervous or uncomfortable talking about? What topics carry stigma or lead to stereotyping?

2. Are topics like mental health, mental illness, race, class, gender, and ability discussed in open and positive ways?

3. How does the staff connect with individual students? How do they build a community within each school and classroom where students feel connected, know each other, and feel that they belong?

4. What is your school doing to build connections and community with families and community members? Do parents feel welcomed into your school? Do community members attend events even though they don't have children there?

IDENTITY

How well do you know your students as individuals? This question focuses us upon the issue of identity. Identity development and formation is a process that encompasses a set of beliefs, attitudes, and values about oneself and the many ways we experience the world of school. Schools are often not organized in ways that constantly consider the individual. Instead, we have created a system where we put students into larger groups or classes by age, ability, or gender. Teachers don't see themselves as teaching individuals but rather talk about teaching classes. This "platoon system" of organizing schools may help manage the millions of students in our schools but it is also a roadblock to knowing an individual student deeply.

Identity development is at the core of human development, especially during the first 20 years of life. Schools play a crucial role in helping individuals determine "Who am I"? This is a period of self-discovery in which the process of growth and maturity occurs in a variety of domains: cognitive, social, emotional, psychological, spiritual, moral. How do I learn? How do I fit in? How do I relate to others? We need to consider and connect social identities related to ethnicity, race, gender, and other social and cultural factors. This *intersectionality* of multiple identities must be understood and addressed by educators and school leaders as they plan curriculum, design systems, develop programs, and determine various policies. They also need to think about how identity development impacts mental health.

Once again, there are many ways for schools to maintain a focus on identity and human development in students. Classroom teachers can shift away from teacher-centered instruction to student-centered instruction, allowing teachers more time to work one-on-one and really get to know kids. These classrooms can also be places where students can explore their identities in safe and respected ways, through class leadership positions, cooperative learning, and choosing elements of the curriculum. Morning meetings and Advisories can also be systems that allow students to explore their identities every day and to interact with other students. Consider how students engage in learning. How ready to learn are they when they enter the classroom? Here is an opportunity to understand not only how they learn but who they are as a learner. Social and emotional learning skills and curricula can also provide opportunities to explore who they are. Finally, the culture and climate of the school can be oriented around student voice and building individual relationships.

DIVERSITY, EQUITY, AND INCLUSION

You can't consider identity without considering that diversity, equity, and inclusion play a major role in student and adult mental health. At the heart of mental health is the experience of belonging as a member of a community. Creating a welcoming community for all students means respecting the diversity of experience and perspectives which provides a rich learning environment for all. Unfortunately, too many obstacles stand in the way of this universal belonging, such as racism, sexism, classism, ableism, and other forms of discrimination. Mental health itself is often the target of bias. We need to expand attention and awareness to neurodiversity and the many different ways students engage and learn. There are multiple factors to consider in the complex web of identity and the intersection with mental health.

Teachers and administrators have the power and capacity to create inclusive and diverse communities in our schools. This begins with being "seen" and included through the correct pronunciation of names to equitable grading practices to celebrating and honoring cultural events. It means acknowledging that different levels of power and privilege exist and then offering ways to navigate that. Students must also see themselves in the curriculum, which means broadening what we have traditionally taught and letting go of some traditional content that is no longer relevant to the next generation. Most importantly, educators must embrace what others like Gloria Ladson-Billings, Gholdy Muhammad, and bell hooks have endorsed for decades: There is a strength in diversity of perspectives, opinions, and experiences that leads to better decisions, creativity, and equitable outcomes. Each of our students brings to school certain assets that must be seen and celebrated in every classroom and school. In designing Wolcott College Prep High School, a successful school in Chicago for students with learning differences, Head of School Miriam Pike flipped the language often used in special education to create a more positive focus on strengths rather than deficits: "I strongly advocate for strength-based models and frameworks, as opposed to the deficit model. We decided to use the term learning differences, which is not without controversy ... The counterpoint to that is that we value all people, the way they are, for whom they are. We're not trying to fix people." To do diversity, equity, and inclusion work is essential to establishing a Tier 1 environment for all students and staff. It is foundational to a mentally healthy classroom and school.

PAUSE AND REFLECT

Take a moment to think, discuss, or write about these questions:

1. Make a list of all the different identities that are represented in your student body and staff. Do you acknowledge all of them? How are they celebrated? Can you point to how each identity is represented in your curriculum? What traditions in your school are acknowledged, celebrated, or omitted?

2. Do you and your colleagues understand *intersectionality*? Is there agreement about what it means and how to use it to support students and staff?

ENVIRONMENTAL RISK AND PROTECTIVE FACTORS

Every context we find ourselves in carries with it certain challenges or risks that might get in the way of safety or learning. When designing learning environments we must consider what risks exist that could impact students and adults. Doing so allows us to better implement Tier 1 strategies. For example, a student who becomes nervous around groups of people may find classrooms with thirty students or crowded hallways during passing periods as overwhelming and stressful. If the school is located in a community with scarce resources or little access to healthy foods, then some students may be coming to school hungry or malnourished. Schools that are located near active train tracks often work with train companies and local public officials to educate young people about staying off the tracks. All of these are potential risk factors that need to be addressed in a Tier 1 plan for mental and physical health.

By addressing risk factors schools can begin to change the way a problem is perceived and see new possibilities for action. We encourage school leaders and leadership teams to do a careful assessment of the potential risks in their school and community when building their Mental Health Action Plan. Understanding risk provides an opportunity to intervene and address the underlying conditions and possible root causes of stressful or unhealthy conditions.

Protective factors in a school environment are positive influences that support healthy development and mental health. They protect the individual from adverse experiences and promote positive outcomes. In the home, supportive family members and parents can be a strong protective factor, as can regular routines, healthy food, and sleep. In the school, protective factors start with every student feeling like they have positive relationships with peers and at least one adult in the school they can go to if they have a problem or question. Access to healthy food and water at school, whether through the regular food service or a free and reduced lunch program, is also an important protective factor. The number of staff dedicated to counseling, social work, or school psychology, as well as regular training of all staff on mental health support, would be another important way of supporting student health. Ultimately, we want our students to thrive. Building protective factors promotes and cultivates resilience and builds capacity for managing challenges.

TECHNOLOGY AND SOCIAL MEDIA

Technology plays a very powerful role in schools and learning. The ability to access information easily, connect people across distance and time, and create remarkable products makes educational technology a useful tool in teaching and learning. Schools have been able to use portable devices and laptops in one-to-one learning, curricular materials, videos, and assessments. At the same time, technology also holds the potential to be misused and wreak havoc. It is constantly changing and at a pace that educators can't always keep up with! In the mental health area, we have seen technology offer amazing advantages like making health information readily available, creating connections and social groups to combat isolation, and deploying applications that can teach mindfulness. Unfortunately, we've also seen cyberbullying, screen addiction, and distraction rise in recent years. Parents see their children on devices in school and at home with many worried about screen time and the potentially negative impact that could have.

Schools must have a clear understanding of all these issues and provide students, staff, and parents with guidelines on how to use technology in positive ways. Research continues to grow on all these issues and we have much more to learn, but we also need to be more sophisticated in understanding technology. For example, research has shown many positive uses of technology over many decades, such as assistive technology in special education, access to information and curricular materials, and in creative endeavors such as writing, art, and STEM. More recently, studies have downplayed the impact of what we call *screen time* and instead are focusing on what young people are doing on their devices. In 2023, the U.S. Surgeon General warned that the use of social media by children and adolescents was a significant health hazard as it exposed young people to misinformation, hate speech, and negative or self-comparison issues that could lead to unhealthy thinking and behaviors (Richtel, 2023). Schools can play a role in helping students by educating them from a young age on the appropriate use of technology. Organizations like Common Sense offer educators and parents great tips on how to use technology in a safe and positive manner. For example, they provide reviews of movies and television shows focusing on age appropriateness. Some of their articles focus on screen time, social media, and online safety (www.commonsensemedia.org).

PAUSE AND REFLECT

Take a moment to think, discuss, or write about these questions:

1. Make a list of the most important risk factors facing your school. What are the protective factors that support students, staff, and families?

2. How are technology and social media used in your school for instructional purposes? Are you teaching members of the school community about how to manage technology in their lives?

TIER 1 INTERVENTIONS

Teaching About the Mind, Body, and Brain

One of the most important interventions we can provide to all students in Tier 1 is teaching them about the mind, body, and brain. Thanks to science, we know a lot about the body and the brain, especially due to the explosion of neuroscience research in the past two decades. Certainly, our bodies undergo the greatest explosions of growth and change during the first 20 years of life. Young people are living through these changes and have lots of questions about their bodies. Health and science courses and curricula should be essential parts of a school's content and be seen as equal to reading, writing, and arithmetic.

Neuroscience explains how the brain works and how it is connected to the central nervous system and our bodily functions. Having a basic understanding of the amygdala and the prefrontal cortex means students will realize how the fight–flight–freeze response in our amygdala gets in the way of our logic center. And how the brain sends signals to other parts of the body, resulting in physiological responses. We will explore this further in the next chapter but certainly teaching about neuroscience should be foundational as a Tier 1 prevention strategy. Integrating an understanding of brain science should be an essential component of staff development.

Learning about neuroscience and the research behind it can help us shift to more optimal ways of managing stress, anxiety, and trauma. Practices that can be taught as coping strategies include mindful breathing, physical movement, engaging in creative arts, mindfulness activities, service learning, and reflective writing. So many of these can be built into regular lesson plans and daily classroom practices so there is the chance to do them many times a day, and so they are embedded in content area learning.

Another important brain–science topic for students and educators alike to understand is neuroplasticity. Neuroplasticity refers to children's brains as being malleable and changeable, rather than fixed. This plasticity can be impacted by learning, environmental factors, and relationships for both good or ill. The brain has an intrinsic and dynamic ability to continually alter its structure and function. For this reason, teachers and administrators must create positive experiences and school environments.

Simple things like orderly passing periods, teachers welcoming students into the classroom with a warm hello or high-five, calm corners in the classroom, or open gym spaces provide students with the kinds of positivity the brain needs to relax and be ready to learn. On the other hand, chaotic cafeterias or hallways, unsupervised bathrooms and locker rooms, tense or anxiety pro-voking classrooms, or lack of access to greenspace can have a negative impact on the brain and lead to heightened stress. The more we can get our brains to make connections and build neurons, the more we build its capacity to learn.

As we understand the function of the brain, we need to consider both students and staff. For example, understanding a concept like mirror neurons in the brain is crucial in the teacher to student relationship (Acharya & Shukla, 2012). These neurons impact how we relate and respond to each other. Our brains pick up on vocal tone, body language, and subtle movements in the muscles of the face. When we experience stress, these are communicated to others around us. If others are stressed, we can become stressed. If someone is calm, then we become calm. We literally "mirror" the other person. So imagine now a student who is stressed out, anxious, or dysregulated in some way. A calm teacher has the opportunity to coregulate with the student. A well-regulated teacher can help a dysregulated student, but a dysregulated teacher can never effectively help a dysregulated student. Knowing more about brain science and the connection between the brain and the body can be crucial knowledge for teachers and a skill we can all learn.

Self-Efficacy and Collective Efficacy

Self-efficacy is the belief in one's self and abilities, those things that help us say "I got this!" Research by people like Albert Bandura (1977, 1997), Carol Dweck (2006), and Angela Duckworth (2016) points to the importance of teaching kids to believe in themselves and their ability to control their lives and actions, as well as to cope with adversity. This is true for both personal decisions that cultivate skills and resilience, like saying no to risky peer pressure or applying for a job, to academics, like finishing a homework assignment or doing well on a test.

Students need to be surrounded by positive messages to improve their self-efficacy but also supportive peers and teachers. Imagine a school where every student felt supported by every adult. Where students gave messages of positivity to each other. Where students and staff turned out in droves to support the basketball team and the chess team equally. All of these would be prevention strategies to help develop good self-efficacy in every student. Students also need support and instruction on developing coping and self-management skills to deal with stress, conflict, and failure, learning to manage in the form of vulnerability and to bounce back and grow.

Adults also benefit from positive self-efficacy, especially teachers and administrators. Researcher John Hattie has found that teacher self-efficacy and collective efficacy both have a significantly positive impact on student learning and experience. Teachers who believe they are individually making a difference in the lives of kids have this positive impact on their own students. More importantly, when an entire staff believes they are helping every kid learn more, student grades and test scores improve (Hattie, 2015).

School structures like professional learning communities (PLCs) and school-wide data analysis days can raise collective efficacy through collaborative discussions of student learning, both what is going well and what we can do better (Donohoo, 2017). Collective efficacy is the recognition that teaching is an emotional practice and that emotions form the basis for a motivation to learn. When we create classrooms that are safe, brave spaces, where positive relationships connect students to each other and adults, we are then building the conditions for a positive sense of self and collective efficacy.

PAUSE AND REFLECT

Take a moment to think, discuss, or write about these questions:

1. Where do students learn about neuroscience in your current curriculum? How could this information be made more common and part of everyday thinking?

2. How would you rate student and staff self-efficacy? What examples can you point to of students and staff showing belief in themselves?

3. Does the entire staff have a good sense of both individual and collective efficacy, and the belief that what they are doing is making a difference? What activities could help build greater collective efficacy?

4. What strategies do you have to prevent and repair harm? How do you help, support, and teach restorative practice that deals with adversity, harm, relationships, or conflict?

Social and Emotional Learning

Attending to the social and emotional dimensions of school is foundational to creating a mentally healthy school. For each individual, social and emotional learning (SEL) teaches life skills such as self-awareness and self-management that are central to developing mental and physical wellness. Psychologist Laurence Steinberg reminds us that the single most important skill that we can teach our children and that predicts social and academic success, and well-being, is the capacity for self-regulation. We also know the power of relationships and living within a community of caring develops coping and resiliency skills, as well as positivity. As the great Yale researcher Dr. James Comer (1995) says, "No significant learning occurs without a significant relationship."

While there are many good SEL frameworks, the most widely used comes from the Collaborative for Academic, Social, and Emotional Learning (CASEL) and includes the following:

- Self-awareness

- Self-management

- Social awareness

- Relationship-building

- Decision-making

Self-awareness refers to the ability to know oneself and to be aware of your own strengths and limitations, as well as the world around you. Self-management is the ability to set goals and create the conditions to achieve them. Social awareness is understanding others and having empathy. Relationship-building is the skill of connecting with others and working collaboratively. Decision-making is thinking through a problem and making a choice of what to do (or not to do!). Each of these are foundational skills that can be learned and practiced by anyone (CASEL, 2022).

Clearly, everyone should have some facility with these skills! Imagine if every adult felt confident in their ability to manage their emotions, develop relationships with others, and make good decisions. But in schools, we don't have to imagine the impact SEL skills have on kids and learning. Study after study shows us that when schools teach SEL skills in a regular, coherent way to kids, they end up learning better and feeling better about their school (Durlak et al., 2011; Greenberg, 2023). The best way to teach any skill is to make it *universal*, which means it shows up in both formal and informal ways throughout a child's school day. It also means explicitly teaching it through classroom lessons, activities, and classroom practices.

There are so many ways schools can support the social and emotional development of students. One is to provide students with an advisor system, which is a period of time every day when staff can check in with students and students can build better relationships with each other. Advisor periods can also be used to deploy an SEL curriculum in your school. Providing students with enough counselors, social workers, psychologists, and nurses is another way the school can support students. These trained educators can offer one on one and group counseling to students and staff. All teachers and school personnel require training in social and emotional learning so they can support every student in the school. When coupled with academic and physical support systems, social and emotional support can result in rising academic success and a more positive school culture and climate.

Of course, the best Tier 1 intervention with SEL is to build skill development into every lesson, every day. This is actually not as difficult as it sounds since most teachers already teach skills like self-awareness, relationship-building, and decision-making. The point is to make it a conscious and explicit purpose of each lesson. Teachers can teach self-awareness and self-management through journal writing, self-evaluations, meditation, and goal-setting. They can teach social awareness and relationship-building through group work, role play, studying historical figures or literary characters, and discussion circles. And students can learn about decision-making through science labs, ethical dilemmas, and independent projects (Dohrer & Golebiewski, 2023).

Any lesson or activity that engages students in learning subject-area content and even one SEL skill is the kind of integration we are looking for in classrooms. If a lesson or activity can attend to more than one SEL skill, that's even better. And there are some practices that involve all five of the SEL skills:

- Project-based learning
- Problem-solving
- Service learning
- Community service
- Restorative circles
- Competitive teams
- Music or theater ensembles
- Teaching others
- Running a business
- Maker education

Another way to integrate SEL into everyday school experience is teaching students about mindfulness practices and how to cultivate emotional balance. Ryan Redman from the Flourish Foundation in Ketchum, Idaho, works with administrators and teachers to implement mindfulness and SEL practices in schools and classrooms. Daily activities like meditation, kinesthetic learning, cooperative learning, and self-reflection all help students manage their emotions, cultivate empathy, and develop mental health resilience. Redman says,

This is really the preventative side of things. In physical health, there are many good things, such as exercise, a good diet, and nutrition, that can support our physical well-being. And the idea with these mindfulness programs is at least on that tier one we can act as a kind of vaccine, where students can kind of inoculate themselves with a number of things that can support themselves as they encounter the adversities in their life, both inwardly and outwardly, that might make them prone to slipping into mental health disorders later on. (Personal interview)

More and more schools are integrating time into the school day and classroom lessons focused on teaching and practicing these important mindfulness skills. They align perfectly with self-awareness and self-management, while also preparing us to make better decisions. They also should be a part of staff culture so adults can reap the benefits of mindfulness.

PAUSE AND REFLECT

Take a moment to think, discuss, or write about these questions:

1. Is there a "common language" across your school about SEL? Do you have an SEL curriculum?

2. How well do you integrate the teaching of SEL skills into each course, especially academic coursework?

3. What are examples of SEL skills that are integrated in the curriculum?

Physical Learning and Wellness

Another foundational area of a whole-person and whole-school approach to mental health is physical health. The health of our body is directly connected to our cognitive, social, and emotional lives. This includes nutrition, hygiene, sleep, environment, and exercise. There should be time for rest, for play, and for movement. All of these can impact a student's ability to understand, comprehend, create, and learn. Adults in our schools—teachers, staff, administrators—must also be attentive to their own physical well-being so they are ready to support students every day. For these reasons, physical health and wellness is an essential building block of a mentally healthy school and should be part of your Tier 1 prevention plan.

If we return again to the basics, it is important to make sure that students and staff have access to healthy food, water, air, and physical surroundings. Many schools have invested in air conditioning, air filtering systems, and updated heating to make sure everyone is breathing in fresh air and staying cool or warm depending on the day. There is plenty of research that points to the importance of green spaces, plants, and access to the outdoors as having a positive impact on our bodies, brains, and emotions, which help us learn better (Horton, 2021). Even seeing plants, bushes, trees, and grass out a window can help, as can plants in a classroom.

Schools have also invested in water-bottle filling stations as they have upgraded drinking fountains so students have ample access to fresh water. And as Tim discovered as a principal, there are a LOT of emotions connected with the quality, cost, and access of food service in a school! When the time came to renew the contract with an outside food provider, it took months of discussions and debates with an array of stakeholders to choose a company that could provide both healthy and tasty food. Healthy food provides students with the sustenance and energy their bodies and brains need to stay focused and happy throughout the day. Tim also oversaw the replacement of drinking fountains with water refilling stations to provide everyone with clean drinking water that also respected the environment. The physical plant of each school building must also be cared for every day. Members of the custodial staff provide an essential role in keeping the school grounds and buildings safe and clean for student learning. Whenever possible, administrators should involve students and families in discussions and decisions related to food, water, and other environmental concerns.

There are also many ways we can support and teach students about physical health and overall wellness. This begins with the curriculum. Your physical education and health curricula should be up to date and offer the most cutting edge information about physical health and wellness. These teachers and staff should seek out high-quality materials and professional learning to provide students with the best instruction in these areas. The science curriculum can also be an important place where students learn about the human body, development, reproduction, genetics, and nutrition.

Before, during, and after-school programs and clubs, such as ultimate frisbee or weightlifting or intramural sports, can provide opportunities for kids to move around and exercise. A school's athletic program should also be aligned with the curriculum of the school in supporting health and wellness. Students should be provided ample opportunities throughout the day for "brain breaks" and physical movement. Finally, the school nurse is an important school leader who can not only recognize individual student needs but also provide support and leadership to the development of curriculum and policies related to physical health.

We want to highlight an element of physical wellness that has a tremendous impact on both students and adults: sleep. Sleep can have both positive and negative effects on our physical and psychological well-being. Study after study shows the importance of sleep on mental health, physical wellness, and overall attitude, something scientists call *sleep health*. There are even studies that delve into the connection between sleep and race, class, and gender, as well as age (Hale et al., 2020; Levy et al., 2016; Miller, 2023; Watson et al., 2015). The National Heart, Lung, and Blood Institute (2023) at the National Institutes of Health recommends that adults get between seven and nine hours of sleep each night and children six to Twelve years old should get nine to twelve hours a night. Sleep is especially important for children as they go through massive physical growth and sleep allows the body to make these metamorphic changes.

Researchers have also found links between our ability to manage stress, anxiety, and trauma with getting enough regular sleep. Administrators and teachers can educate themselves, students, and parents on the importance of sleep. The National Sleep Foundation (2023) recommends that everyone should exercise 30 minutes a day, spend time in bright light during the day, and eat meals at consistent times. At night, we should avoid late night snacks, caffeine, and electronic devices leading up to bedtime. And while the amount of sleep is important, it can be more important to have a consistent bedtime in an environment conducive to deep sleep. All this can be taught to students and offered as professional learning for both staff and parents.

One way of enacting Tier 1 prevention on health and wellness is by instituting an All-School Wellness Team. This is a way to bring together stakeholders from across a school or district to maintain a systems-level view of health and wellness efforts, but also connect individuals so that work can be coordinated. At one school, the principal chairs the team along with a few other key administrators. It includes teacher leaders representing content areas like health, physical education, science, and any other teachers interested. Athletics and activities are also represented by the staff leading those teams and clubs that do work in the wellness area. The school nurse and social worker are important members of this team. Students and parents are also represented through student council and parent organizations. Finally, members of the custodial, cafeteria, and school safety staff are also essential members of the team. They meet once a month to share around the table the activities each of them is working on and to shape policy across the school and district. Often, outside school organizations will come and present to the team so their efforts can be coordinated with the school. An All-School Wellness Team like this would be a very simple yet powerful Tier 1 strategy for any school to implement.

Take a moment to think, discuss, or write about these questions:

1. Where in your curriculum do you explicitly teach students about physical wellness, such as healthy eating, sleep, exercise, and mindfulness?

2. What programs or systems are in place that provide students with healthy food, water, air, and access to the outdoors?

Academic and Cognitive Learning

Schools are first and foremost institutions of learning. Students spend most of their time in schools in classes or receiving academic help. There are lots of ways the academic program and academic philosophy of a school can impact student mental health. The school's philosophy about learning, as well as our approach to curriculum, instruction, and assessment, must be in line with the school's goals regarding mental health.

This includes a number of related issues, such as lesson planning, classroom management, classroom environment, teacher availability, use of time, homework, and academic resource centers. All these and more impact learning for every student in every classroom.

One of the challenges of the traditional school approach to learning is a one-size-fits-all model. This approach was essential in the 20th century for the rapid expansion of universal K–12 education in the United States as we adopted the "platoon system" of teaching groups of students, often large groups, to manage the sheer number of young people going to school. In the name of efficiency, we also turned to a narrow conception of learning and of teaching, one that focused on behaviorism. All students were taught the same lesson, often using a single form of instruction like "I do, we do, you do," and the content from a single perspective or cultural point of view. If an assessment could measure a change in knowledge, then the student had "learned." In time, we learned much more about how learning occurs in the brain and how learning is impacted by sociocultural forces. We may have improved the number of students who could access schools, but we haven't increased the number of students who can access the content. There is still much work to be done on making learning, teaching, content, and assessment accessible to all kinds of learners.

Universal Design for Learning (UDL) is one of the best interventions we can initiate in a mentally healthy classroom. UDL changes teaching and learning from a one-size-fits-all model to a universal model. Content comes from multiple sources and connects to an array of perspectives and identities. Students learn content and skills through multiple strategies, often chosen by the student. Student understanding and learning are demonstrated by many means, again often chosen by the student. UDL not only engages each learner in the process of learning but also gives them a chance to explore and represent their learning in many ways. As such, a teacher's lesson plan is much more student-centered, resulting in a classroom setting that is immediately more comfortable and engaging for students.

Our understanding of how stress, anxiety, and trauma get in the way of learning is also important to designing classrooms and systems that support learning. In order to learn algebra or U.S. history or vocabulary in Spanish, a student's brain must be "available," which means the amygdala is not engaged in the flight–fight–freeze response, and the prefrontal cortex is ready to provide logical analysis and comprehension. Certainly, teachers should look for opportunities to teach about the brain, especially in the context of their own content area.

But more importantly, teachers have the power to shape the classroom environment and create the conditions in which *every* student feels comfortable, safe, engaged, and ready to learn. This begins with the physical arrangement of the classroom. Has it been designed for student-centered learning? For collaboration? In an elementary classroom, moving away from rows and toward learning stations can make a big difference. Is there space in your room for morning and afternoon meetings as a class and for activities like reading, math, or guest speakers? In middle school and high school classrooms, how are you arranging desks to create small groups or circles? You may have space to include areas for collaboration, quiet independent reading, or for a "calm corner," which is a desk or space that can offer some level of privacy a student could use to calm themselves and regulate their emotions.

Learning can also be impacted by how we operate the classroom, something we previously called *classroom management*. Many teachers stand outside their classroom door or just inside the door to welcome students into the space with a greeting or special handshake. Regular structures and order are often much better for students who are managing stress, anxiety, or trauma. Or some students might need to be energized as they come in, maybe with an immediate activity or some music playing. Teachers may want to build in a few minutes for relationship-building or meditation to help focus attention and get students ready to learn.

Maximizing instructional time is also important as it provides structure and puts learning front and center in what happens in the classroom. The more organized a teacher is, the more time that can be spent on learning activities rather than administration. It is also critically important to engage in a collaborative effort to define classroom rules, guidelines, and procedures. Students need to have a say in what happens in the room, as does the teacher! It also provides students with important structure and reduces uncertainty. Finally, think through how certain processes and assumptions about competition, deadlines, and activities might generate stress or anxiety in students. Some things, like deadlines, will need to happen but often we ramp up these to the point where they generate unnecessary stress and anxiety. Classrooms that focus on revision, group work, portfolios, reflection, and standards-based grading help reduce some of those traditional approaches that often are more about completing tasks than learning.

At the broader school or district level, administrators and educators need to think about how school policies might impact mental health. The first place to look is your Student Handbook and the policies related to things like attendance, tardiness, behavior, and discipline. We are coming out of a period in schooling where zero-tolerance policies have led to an increase in expulsions and out-of-school suspensions. The philosophy has been to exclude a student from class and let the administration handle it, or to completely ban someone from school. In an effort to reduce the school-to-prison pipeline, many states have started pushing for a change in paradigm to more restorative practices. Better to work with the student and the entire class community on whatever happened within the classroom than removing them from the learning environment. We'll explore this a bit later in Tier 2 but certainly maintaining classroom rules that keep students in the room are better than those that remove them, at least for most situations.

School leaders should also take a look at their entire discipline system and think about whether the rules as written are helping or harming students, especially those that are struggling with mental health or external factors beyond their control. We need to move away from a perspective that asks "What is wrong with you?" to one that asks "What is happening to you?" We should ask what are *your* needs, *your* strengths, and how can we support *you*? Our goal should always be to find ways of returning kids to the classroom where they can continue to learn academic content and skills.

PAUSE AND REFLECT

Take a moment to think, discuss, or write about these questions:

1. In what ways is the instruction in your school focused on the teacher or focused on student learning? Who is doing "the work" of learning: your teachers or your students?

2. How many of your teachers are utilizing a Universal Design for Learning (UDL) approach to lessons, activities, and assessments?

3. What are teachers doing to create engaging, welcoming classroom environments?

4. Are your grading or discipline policies punitive or restorative? How do they support the individual needs of every student?

EVERYTHING RESTS ON THE FOUNDATION OF TIER 1

A multitiered systems of support model relies on a strong first tier of support. In our mental health model, Tier 1 is by far the most important. It represents the solid foundation that we want to establish for every student and every adult in our schools. It is also the way that we frontload prevention so we can reduce the amount of intervention and response needed later.

After reading through this chapter, imagine your school being deeply focused on every one of these Tier 1 strategies. Imagine a school where every student who walks in the door feels welcomed, at home, cared for, and ready to learn. Imagine them walking through a hallway where kids are smiling, and are being recognized by their first name by teachers and staff, where they see artwork and writing from their peers. When they walk into their classroom, the teacher has welcomed them, and they see peers who they know are going to support them even when they make mistakes. They are in a classroom where they not only feel comfortable but they also know they are going to learn something amazing today. Imagine a school where students have a variety of choices in extracurricular activities that meet their interests and their needs. Where teachers are engaged in regular professional learning communities and are constantly getting better from year one to year thirty. A place where parents gather together to work collaboratively with the school to learn about child development and parenting and learning.

If we established this as the new normal in every school, there's no question that we would see improvement in overall school culture and school climate but mostly in student learning, as well as an overall sense of well-being. It would radically reduce the number of people finding themselves in crisis or and it would increase each person's ability to cope and be resilient and find real positivity.

This is not some kind of pipe dream. It's very possible in the schools that we have today. The difference maker would be rethinking how we "do school" with this baseline of mental health. Very practically speaking, it would mean pulling together all stakeholders in the school to do an immediate audit of what they are already doing well and in alignment with this vision. Then an honest gap analysis should be undertaken to determine what needs to be changed or done better to achieve this vision. These would be hard conversations and they would benefit from having as many voices speaking as possible, but, again, this is not impossible! Coming out of these kinds of conversations, a school would then have the blueprint for an action plan that they could begin to implement immediately and long term to achieve this vision of mental health at Tier 1.

Both of us have taught in and worked with schools that have done this kind of work and the results are truly amazing. And as we will see in the next two chapters, building this foundation is crucial to creating the kind of Tier 2 and

Tier 3 interventions that are required for supporting *all* students and staff in moments of crisis or for those individuals who need additional support to achieve their potential and their goals.

A school that looks like this, that truly attended to these Tier 1 issues, and created foundational strategies that supported all learners, all people, all the time would be immediately better in supporting our mental health. We would find ourselves in a place where we could be our true selves, to find support in both our victories and our failures. And as each of us grapples with the normal stress, anxiety, and trauma in life, we would be able to do so in an environment that made that struggle easier and allow us to reengage in normal life much faster. How we do this for each individual in the school community will be the test for whether our Tier 1 prevention plan is successful.

CREATING YOUR MENTAL HEALTH ACTION PLAN

Take some time to work with your school-based team to think through the following elements of your comprehensive Mental Health Action Plan. The full plan template is located in Appendix A.

Prevention and Early Intervention Plan: Tier I

1. What are we doing for <u>all</u> students?

2. How do we develop culture?

3. How do we get to know each individual?

4. How do we build relationships?

5. How do we measure school climate?

6. How regularly do we collect and analyze school climate data?

7. How do we use school climate data to drive policy decisions, structures, and processes?

8. How do we offer academic support <u>in</u> classes?

9. How do we offer academic support <u>outside</u> of classes?

10. How do we offer physical health support?

11. How do we offer social and emotional support?

12. How is SEL integrated in our academic program? Cocurricular and extracurricular activities? Athletics?

13. Do we have foundational support and a plan for SEL that strengthens <u>adult</u> capacity and competence and promotes SEL for all students?

14. How do we approach student behavior? What are our disciplinary policies?

15. Do we have restorative justice practices in our school culture?

16. What would it take for us to change the mindset and skillset of our staff to a restorative justice approach?

REFERENCES

Acharya, S., & Shukla, S. (2012). Mirror neurons: Enigma of the metaphysical modular brain. *Journal of Natural Science, Biology and Medicine, 3*(2), 118–124.

Bandura, A. (1977). Self-efficacy: Toward a unifying theory of behavioral change. *Psychological Review, 84*(2), 191–215.

Bandura, A. (1997). *Self-efficacy: The exercise of control.* W. H. Freeman.

CASEL. (2022). *What is the CASEL Framework?* https://casel.org/fundamentals-of-sel/what-is-the-casel-framework/

Center for Success in High-Needs Schools. http://www.center4success.com

Cohen, S., Doyle, W. J., Skoner, D. P., Rabin, B. S., & Gwaltney, J. M. (1997). Social ties and susceptibility to the common cold. *JAMA, 277*(24), 1940–1944. https://doi.org/10.1001/jama.1997.03540480040036

Comer, J. (1995). *Lecture given at Education Service Center.* Region IV.

Common Sense Media. (n.d.). www.commonsensemedia.org

Dohrer, T., & Golebiewski, T. (2023). Integrating social and emotional learning into classroom practice. *Voices for Educational Equity, 19*(1), 11–19.

Donohoo, J. (2017). *Collective efficacy: How educators' beliefs impact student learning.* Corwin.

Duckworth, A. (2016). *Grit: The power of passion and perseverance* (1st ed.). Scribner.

Durlak, J., Weissberg, R., Dymnicki, A., Taylor, R., & Schellinger, K. (2011). The impact of enhancing students' social and emotional learning: A meta-analysis of school-based universal interventions. *Child Development, 82,* 405–432.

Dweck, C. S. (2006). *Mindset: The new psychology of success.* Random House.

Greenberg, M. T. (2023, March 6). *Evidence for social and emotional learning in schools.* Learning Policy Institute. https://learningpolicyinstitute.org/product/evidence-social-emotional-learning-schools-report

Hale, L., Troxel, W., & Buysse, D. (2020). Sleep health: An opportunity for public health to address health equity. *Annual Review of Public Health, 41*(1), 81–99.

Hattie, J. (2015). The applicability of visible learning to higher education. *Scholarship of Teaching and Learning in Psychology, 1*(1), 79–91.

Horton, T. (2021). Nature connections and social emotional learning. In *Evolutionary and ecological approaches to health and development.* Northwestern University. https://www.nhlbi.nih.gov/health/sleep

Hwang, T.-J., Rabheru, K., Peisah, C., Reichman, W., & Ikeda, M. (2020). Loneliness and social isolation during the COVID-19 pandemic. *International Psychogeriatrics, 32*(10), 1217–1220.

Learning Policy Institute and Turnaround for Children. (2021). *Design principles for schools: Putting the science of learning and development into action.* https://learningpolicyinstitute.org/sites/default/files/product-files/SoLD_Design_Principles_Principle_3_Rich_Learning.pdf

Levy, D., Heissel, J., Richeson, J., & Adam, E. (2016). Psychological and biological responses to race-based social stress as pathways to disparities in educational outcomes. *American Psychologist, 71*(6), 455–473.

Miller, N. (2023). Sleep disparities: An explainer and research roundup. *The Journalist's Resource.* https://journalistsresource.org/home/racial-disparities-in-sleep/

National Heart, Lung, and Blood Institute. (2023). *How sleep works.* https://www.nhlbi.nih.gov/health/sleep-deprivation

National Sleep Foundation. (2023). *How does exercise influence sleep?* Redman, Flourish Foundation in Ketchum. https://www.sleepfoundation.org/physical-activity/best-time-of-day-to-exercise-for-sleep

Richtel, M. (2023, March 21). The surgeon general's new mission: Adolescent mental health. *The New York Times*. https://www.nytimes.com/2023/03/21/health/surgeon-general-ado-lescents-mental-health.html

Watson, N., Badr, M., Belenky, G., Bliwise, D., Buxton, O., Buysse, D., Dinges, D., Gangwisch, J., Grandner, M., Kushida, C., Malhotra, R., Martin, J., Patel, S., Quan, S., & Tasali, E. (2015). Recommended amount of sleep for a healthy adult: A joint consensus statement of the American Academy of Sleep Medicine and Sleep Research Society. *Journal of Clinical Sleep Medicine, 11*(6), 591–592.

CHAPTER 4

....

TIER 2 ISSUES AND INTERVENTIONS FOR STUDENTS, TEACHERS, AND PARENTS ... AND SCHOOLS!

Schools are a key socializing institution in modern societies. They are generally the most important socializing institutions outside of the family. You can change cultural habits effectively by changing what is happening in the process of socialization of the next generation.
—Kay Pranis, leading expert on circles and restorative practices

In a traditional Multitiered Systems of Support (MTSS), Tier 2 is designed to support up to 15% of students in terms of academic or behavioral support, thereby keeping the support being offered cost effective and high quality. These are traditionally targeted interventions to specific students for a short amount of time. As we have thought about mental health support, we actually see Tier 2 as something much more than that.

Universal Tier 1 interventions offer support to ALL students and provide a solid foundation of skill development. When thinking about the broad range of mental health, we assume that at some point every student and staff member will also require some Tier 2 support. We all have moments where we face a challenge or stress or some kind of crisis. It happens when we encounter some content that challenges us or a difficult interaction with a peer, a loss, or a family member falling ill. In a continuum of care approach, Tier 2 interventions are intentionally designed to support students and adults over a short amount of time as they cope with specific situations or events and to change behavior to more positive prosocial behaviors. In this way, Tier 2 needs to be designed for everyone but not everyone at the same time.

We also have some students who require support more often than other students. This is closer to the traditional approach in MTSS where maybe 15% of students and staff need additional help and on a more regular basis. Some of these students have individualized education plans (IEPs) or 504 plans and receive academic and behavioral interventions every day or throughout the week. Others are students who need several weeks of support as they work through a physical or mental issue, like a broken leg or loss of a family member. Schools must design systems that can provide this level of help beyond Tier 1 to help them as well.

School leaders need to assume that at some point their school or community is going to face a crisis. It is not a matter of "if" but "when." If we have designed excellent Tier 1 supports and interventions, then the number of Tier 2 interventions at the school level will be minimal, but they still need to be integrated and performed at an optimal level of excellence. Academic support centers, social workers, family/parent workshops, student affinity groups, restorative justice circles, bullying and harassment training, and peer mediation are all examples of Tier 2 interventions that school leaders can employ to support whole-school mental health support.

In this chapter, you will learn about the science behind some of the forces that tend to result in the most Tier 2 problems that students and staff face each day. Our biggest focus will be on stress, anxiety, and trauma. We'll define these concepts and look at both the internalized and externalized behaviors of students, as well as how they impact the mind, body, brain, and relationships. Then we'll delve into specific prevention and interventions strategies that teachers, administrators, and schools can offer. In the end, you'll be able to design a Tier 2 prevention and intervention strategy as part of your overall Mental Health Action Plan.

TIER 1 AND TIER 2 SCREENERS: BUILDING AN EARLY DETECTION SYSTEM

Before we dive into the challenges facing students and staff, let's talk about the ways a mentally healthy school can identify problems early. We've already established that deep, caring relationships between students and their peers and adults is a critical Tier 1 step. It is also an important screener for Tier 2 issues. In schools where the phrase "If you see something, say something" has been accepted, students are more apt to talk to a teacher or administrator about things that they have seen or heard or felt in and out of school. They are more willing to go to a social worker about a friend who is struggling with eating or suicidal ideation. They are more active in pressing for changes to school policies or better food in the cafeteria or creating a resource center for second-language speakers.

Teachers are often the first to notice issues that students are grappling with so they need to be trained on what the early signs are for stress, anxiety, and trauma. And what to do when they notice something is not right. Administrators who have true open-door policies receive much more feedback from students, staff, and families before or in the early moments of a crisis. Some schools have also had great success with anonymous tip phone numbers, email or text boxes, or even the old-fashioned physical suggestion box. All of these are possible in a culture of caring where real trust, relational trust, exists between all members of the school community.

The other tool to improve your early detection system is the use of actual screeners like school climate surveys, individual response forms, and interviews. School climate surveys, often part of a Tier 1 approach, can give you a broad sense of what is going well in your school, and what needs to be attended to in terms of problems. National surveys like the Centers for Disease Control's Youth Risk Behavior Survey not only give you local data on student attitudes and risk behaviors, but also comparative data from schools across the country (https://www.cdc.gov/healthyyouth/data/yrbs/index.htm). Follow up surveys can begin to pinpoint where you need to intervene or create some kind of Tier 2 response. So can focus groups and individual interviews with students, staff, and parents.

Individual screeners ask students to identify themselves by name so teachers and leaders can intervene on behalf of individuals. While these need to be done carefully to protect privacy, they can be important tools for building an early prevention and intervention system. As we will see later, the adverse childhood experiences (ACE) questionnaire can be a valuable screener for understanding the impact of trauma on a student. However, it should only be used by trained social workers or psychologists and should never be given to groups of students.

There are a number of ways software can be used to collect feedback on student and staff emotions. One example is StrengthenU developed by former principal Jeff McLellan. This very customizable application asks respondents to identify their current emotional state using emojis or an emotion wheel. Next, the app prompts them to quickly write one thing they are grateful or thankful for. Finally, it provides them with a very short lesson about social and emotional learning with an optional prompt they can respond to and save. In just one or two minutes, this app engages respondents in self-awareness, self-reflection, and learning about SEL. Then, the data can be sent to the classroom teacher (anonymously or not) who can see on a dashboard real-time data on students. There is even the opportunity to visualize the emotion data in an "emoji cloud" so the teacher or even the entire class can see how the group is feeling right now, opening the door to rich conversations as a community about how we are doing and where we want to go next. And the text that has been entered by the student can be reviewed by the student individually or with the teacher as they look at their growth in the area of social and emotional learning.

Take a moment to think, discuss, or write about these questions:

1. How do you know a student is struggling in or out of school? What are the signs?

2. What staff development programs do you have to ensure that staff know how to recognize early signs and symptoms of mental health concerns?

3. How do you screen for early identification of potential problems and student concerns?

INTERNALIZED BEHAVIORS: STRESS, ANXIETY, AND TRAUMA

In Tier 1, we suggested that teaching about the brain and neuroscience was important content everyone should learn about. By understanding how the brain works and how our mind, body, and brain respond to normal stress, anxiety, and trauma, each of us can understand ways of coping and responding to these negative forces and allow the prefrontal cortex to recenter itself and make better decisions. Knowing how the brain works, the mind–body–brain connection, will impact our health, well-being, and learning. We also saw how social and emotional learning skills can help us understand academic content better, improve our relationships, and create balance within ourselves to achieve our goals. These SEL skills also have a profound impact on our brains and bodies, helping to bring us back to a place of calm, balance, and regulation. Our physical response to moments of stress, anxiety, and trauma is pretty similar across those areas, although there are also some differences between them. To better understand this response and to design systems of support for each, let's delve more deeply into each of them and the neuroscience behind them.

What Is Stress?

Acclaimed researcher Hans Seyle defined *stress* as the wear and tear upon the body and the brain. The stress response is an embodied response. It affects us physiologically as well as psychologically. With Tier 1 we focused upon universal strategies and a broad understanding of stress, stressors, and the stress response. But there are a number of different ways of framing stress: distress, acute stress, cumulative stress, chronic stress, toxic stress, traumatic stress, and posttraumatic stress. As we will see, the stress response is encoded in our evolutionary DNA which relates to the fight–flight–freeze response and protective mechanism. Anytime we feel threat or danger the stress response is activated. To better understand this stress response, let's take a moment to consider the major regions of the brain.

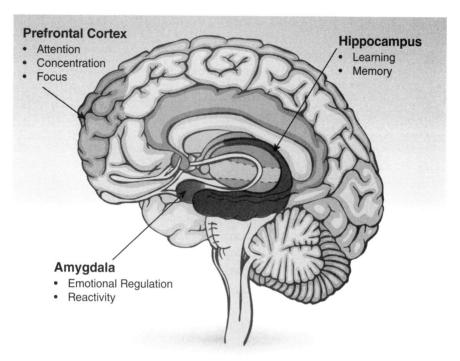

Prefontal Cortex
- Attention
- Concentration
- Focus

Hippocampus
- Learning
- Memory

Amygdala
- Emotional Regulation
- Reactivity

SOURCE: Istock.com/pukrufus

The hippocampus is sometimes referred to as the storage cabinet or memory bank of the brain. It houses short-term or working memory which allows us to integrate new information with previous schema and turn knowledge that has meaning and relevance into long-term memories. The amygdala, the emotional center that is sometimes referred to as the fire alarm of the brain, modulates, modifies, and manages emotional processing. It's designed to react to threats or danger to keep us safe. The amygdala processes distress signals directly from the brain to the rest of the body in the form of the stress hormone cortisol. Cognitive functions such as learning, decision-making, and problem-solving stop and lead to the fight–flight–freeze response. In terms of our evolution, the newest part of the brain layer is in the frontal lobe, sometimes referred to as the CEO of the brain, which manages executive functioning. It is the control center of the brain and overseas executive functioning, working memory, rational thinking, problem-solving, focused attention, organization, and self-regulation.

Keep in mind that the brain is embodied and these three critical regions of the brain do not work in isolation but are interdependent. They communicate by sending electromagnetic and chemical messages to the body's nervous system. This structure connects the brain to the spinal cord, and its primary task is to keep the body alive. It controls automatic bodily functions such as breathing, blood circulation, heart rate, and digestion. When the amygdala senses danger, it activates the stress response through the sympathetic nervous system. Our pupils dilate and heartbeat increases as cortisol is released throughout the body. We are on high alert, ready for anything, and not easily engaging the prefrontal cortex. When the danger is passed or we have successfully brought the prefrontal cortex back online, the parasympathetic nervous system signals to the body that it is time to "rest and digest," to slow the heartbeat, stimulate digestion, and contract our pupils. In this way, the body and brain work in tandem to constantly scan our surroundings, assess whether we are safe or in danger, and then respond. This stress response is encoded into our evolutionary DNA and has helped keep us safe for thousands of years.

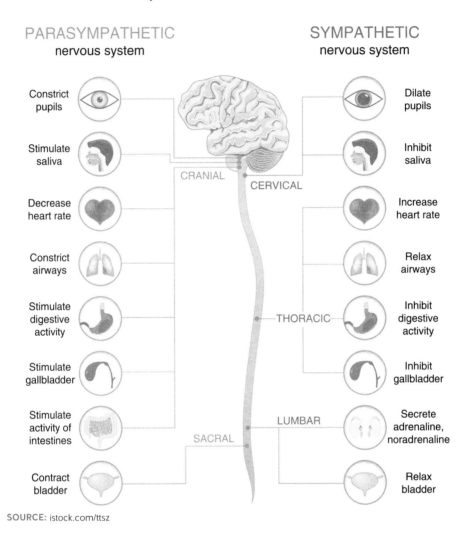

SOURCE: istock.com/ttsz

The Brain Is a Work in Progress

Consider the brain as a complex management system and learning machine. It is also the only social organ in the body. It reads our internal workings, how the various organs in the body work together, but it also reads the environment around us. We are hardwired for survival and we're hardwired for connection. The brain records information through experience and then changes itself so it knows what situations to avoid and what situations to seek out. It uses culture to make sense of the world. Culture is like software to the brain, allowing the hardwire connections to make sense and grow.

The brain is malleable. It adapts to demands and information and the people around us. This is the concept of neuroplasticity, which refers to the brain's ability to grow and form new neural connections and circuits between brain cells, between nerve cells within the brain (Schaefer et al., 2017). Malleability is influenced by experience. Plasticity opens the brain's window to the outside world. This can be both positive and negative. If it is exposed to positive experiences and a healthy environment, the brain can flourish. If the environment is toxic, it can suffer. Malleability permits change for better or worse. Over the past 20 years, scientists have learned quite a bit about the brain and we know that we can significantly change the way the brain works by paying attention to how our nervous system responds to daily life. We know that our day-to-day life is impacted by whether or not our survival responses are activated and having a basic understanding of the automatic survival responses puts us in a better position to work with our nervous system rather than against it. Making the nervous system your ally is the first step to notice what it is telling you and the state you are in.

One additional idea to consider is that anytime we experience stress we experience an emotion. Emotions are experienced in physiological changes the physiological changes that communicate our feelings and how we are responding to something internally or in the world around us. When we feel stress, it is often useful to identify our emotions in order to understand how we are feeling and to reengage the prefrontal cortex. We have to "name it to tame it." Naming the emotion we are feeling engages the prefrontal cortex, the logic center of our brain, and helps us manage the emotion, and therefore our bodily stress response. Being more in touch with our feelings, our body, and our mind leads to better resilience and coping when the stress response is triggered.

Impact of Stress

Thanks to the stress response, some levels of stress can keep us alert to dangers and can prepare our response to an event. We also know that each individual responds differently to various levels of stress. Some of us can cope better than others! As we saw in Tier 1, everyone should be taught the skills to cope with low-level, everyday stress. However, if stress begins to overwhelm our coping skills or the amount of stress is just too much, we may find stress getting in the way of our ability to respond. We may see students become agitated. Or we might see students shut down. Stress can also begin to wear and tear on a student or educator over time, resulting in health-related illnesses or exhaustion. Left unchecked or unsupported, stress can have a severe impact upon physical health and well-being.

Over the last decade, the American Psychological Association (APA, 2022) has tracked reported levels of stress among all Americans through its "Stress in America" report. Regularly, a third of Americans ages 18 and above say stress is overwhelming on most days, with younger Americans reporting higher levels. In children and adolescents, the APA reports that they are as stressed as adults. Yet young people are still developing key coping and resilience skills. Young people need to be taught about stress so they better understand it. We also need to create better screening tools and early intervention systems to know and respond to Tier 1 and Tier 2 stressors and stress in children. As we will see later, we also need to create programs and conditions that teach students and adults how to manage stress, learn mindfulness, and cultivate emotional balance.

PAUSE AND REFLECT

Take a moment to think, discuss, or write about these questions:

1. Does your school have a clear definition and understanding of stress?

2. Where are students being taught about the different regions of the brain and how they act together with the nervous system to create a response in our bodies?

3. Think about the context of your school. What elements of your environment are stressors that might trigger the stress response in students and adults?

What Is Anxiety?

Anxiety is a feeling of worry, nervousness, or unease typically about an imminent event or an outcome that is uncertain or dangerous. It is an alerting signal that something important to us and our welfare needs attention. Anxiety in and of itself isn't a problem; it's a typical, normal response to stress. Often it mobilizes us and can be helpful. For example, when a student has an upcoming exam, some anxiousness can increase cortisol levels and motivate the student to prepare and study. It can also get our mind, body, and brain ready. However, if anxiety is too intense or lasts too long or occurs too frequently, we might be in danger of developing an *anxiety disorder*. Psychologically, these are defined as a nervous disorder characterized by a stage of excessive uneasiness, apprehension, typically with compulsive behaviors and panic attacks. Some people also may perceive situations as being threatening that are actually not. The difference between normal anxiety and acute anxiety is whether the anxiousness is getting in the way of day-to-day living.

Anxiety among young people has been on the rise for over a decade. According to the Centers for Disease Control (CDC), anxiety among children increased from 6.4% in 2012 to 9.4% in 2019. Unfortunately, only 6 in 10 children with anxiety receive treatment (CDC, 2023). There are a number of stress and anxiety disorders to identify generalized anxiety disorder, specific phobias, social phobia, obsessive compulsive disorder, panic disorder, posttraumatic stress disorders. Symptoms of an anxiety attack may include the following:

- Overwhelming fear

- Sense of helplessness

- Feelings of grave danger

- A surge of gloom and doom

- An urgency to escape

- Dizziness

- Shortness of breath

- Numbing, tingling sensations in our extremities

Anxiety- and stress-related disorders are complicated processes that involve our biochemistry, genetics, life experience, and emotions. The interplay of these factors can explain why a stressful experience might trigger anxiety in some students but not in others.

Recognizing the symptoms of anxiety is an important skill to teach children, teens, and adults. Teaching coping strategies will provide opportunities to help students develop adaptive behaviors. By focusing upon early intervention and screening we can also recognize when stress and anxiety becomes a significant issue and a mental health problem. Anxiety disorders are often the earliest mental health disorders that appear in childhood and adolescence. Recognizing these disorders is critical so they don't progress into more significant disorders. Learning coping skills and adaptive strategies to monitor, modify, and manage can be an effective Tier 2 intervention.

School Refusal

One of the biggest ways educators see anxiety in students is school refusal. School refusal is a condition that affects roughly 2% to 5% of children who refuse to come to school due to anxiety or depression. It can be relatively mild and seen in very young students, especially those attending school for the first time, as separation anxiety. Or it can be more severe when students miss school for days, weeks, or even months because they are so anxious about some aspect of school. It is important to recognize that school refusal is not the same as ditching school or truancy, or as life situations such as homelessness or pregnancy. The presenting issue is often avoidant behaviors, often the result of anxiety, such as social anxiety, separation anxiety, or performance anxiety, both real or perceived. The underlying diagnosis of school refusal may be defensive, an escape from threatening situations, or an attempt to gain attention from parents and caregivers.

All behavior has meaning and is a form of communication. As noted previously, understanding the motive and meaning of the behavior, the message that is communicated, and what needs are not being met or skills that need to be developed is key to developing an intervention for a student. Schools should have policies and procedures in place for working with students with school refusal so they are treated equitably and fairly. Parents are likely to benefit from support as well. A collaborative, team-oriented approach will include engaging and offering support for parents in order to manage attendance expectations. It should also include consultation with medical professionals.

When having missed school for an extended period of time, a reentry plan will be essential and should include key staff members who can create a supportive, safe haven in the school for student to work from, as well as structures and routines that address the particular needs of the individual student, particularly those with severe anxiety or depression. These supports include helping the student and families with routines and expectations, teaching and integrating skills that address strategies and skills, attending to and providing academic support and interventions, and consultation with the student's teachers and support staff.

PAUSE AND REFLECT

Take a moment to think, discuss, or write about these questions:

1. Does your school have a clear definition and understanding of anxiety?

2. Think about the context of your school. What elements of your environment might cause anxiety for students and adults?

3. What is your school's process for managing incidents of school refusal?

What Is Trauma?

Trauma is systems overload. Its symptoms are multidimensional and multi-faceted. Working with trauma is working with stress. It can impact normal developmental processes and interrupt the architecture of the brain and the whole nervous system with long-term impact. A traumatic event can seriously disrupt an individual student and normal school routines. It threatens a person's feelings of safety and well-being.

Traumatic events can include an array of events such as violence, natural disasters, illness, accidents, death, and forms of separation. The U.S. Department of Health and Human Services (2014) defines *trauma* in this way: "Individual trauma results from an event, series of events, or set of circumstances that is experienced by an individual as physically or emotionally harmful or life threatening and that has lasting adverse effects on the individual's functioning and mental, physical, social, emotional, or spiritual well-being" (Bethune, 2014). Trauma is measured based on the event's magnitude, complexity, intensity, frequency, and duration of potential stressors. Events in and of themselves are not necessarily traumatic. They become traumatic when they overwhelm and exceed our capacity to cope, when we experience vulnerability and helplessness.

Trauma must be understood from multiple angles, including the event, the experience, and the effect. There are multiple kinds of acute trauma events that we might experience ourselves or witness. One category of trauma events would be through nature. Earthquakes, tornados, hurricanes, floods, blizzards, or excessive heat can all impact our lives directly or indirectly. We have worked with administrators at schools where portions of the school were destroyed due to tornados or high winds. While no one was physically hurt, these weather events traumatized some members of the school community both young and old. The school also had to recover from the damage for weeks.

Another type of trauma event is violence in the form of bullying, fights, physical abuse, or shootings. Certainly, physical or psychological violence causes an immediate stress response and possibly physical harm. However, students and staff can also be impacted by the possibility of violence or by witnessing violence. Serious illness, accidents, loss, and death can also be traumatic. The school we both worked in dealt with a steam-pipe accident that killed a custodian and injured two others. While the connection to the student population was minimal, a few students with previous trauma histories were triggered and distraught over hearing of the death, and of course the staff was deeply affected, particularly the custodial staff.

We also need to recognize that major lifestyle changes and transitions, such as relocating to a new community, starting a new school, changing a teacher, or family dysfunction, can also trigger a trauma response. For example, if a family in your school experiences a major fire in their home, they will encounter a series of stressors that may make the event traumatic for a child in that family.

Children can experience a wide range of responses to a traumatic event, both short term and long term. Shock and denial are typical responses. These events can often generate secondary adversities, life changes, and distress in the child's life. We might see changes in cognition, increased risk-taking, anxiety, or extreme mood swings. Consider that trauma may always "be in the room" whether we see it or not. Coping depends on age, level of development, how students experience the traumatic event, and how they express their lingering distress. Trauma can be REAL or PERCEIVED. Trauma can be RECENT or DISTANT. A crisis stretches our capacity to cope; trauma overwhelms our capacity to cope. In any trauma situation, we also must consider the short-term and long-term effects of directly or indirectly experiencing trauma.

The mind–body–brain connection and the stress response are essential to understanding the physiological impact of trauma on ourselves and on young people. Trauma impacts the whole nervous system. It gets under our skin and affects our physiological health and well-being. It can adversely affect the body as well as brain development. It can have long-term impact on the nervous system where someone can be triggered and shut down. It can affect relationships and learning. Trauma occurs in context, not in isolation. It is important to understand the impact it can have on the individual and also on the system—the classroom, the building, the community.

The Window of Tolerance

The *Window of Tolerance* is a metaphor developed by Dr. Dan Siegel (1999) that can be helpful when thinking about trauma. Siegel refers to an optimal zone of functioning and opposite zone of arousal, where too much or too little can impact our capacity to manage and cope with the challenges of daily life. The graphic below is a way of visualizing and understanding the range in which we may find balance between dysregulation and to be able to utilize the skills to cope.

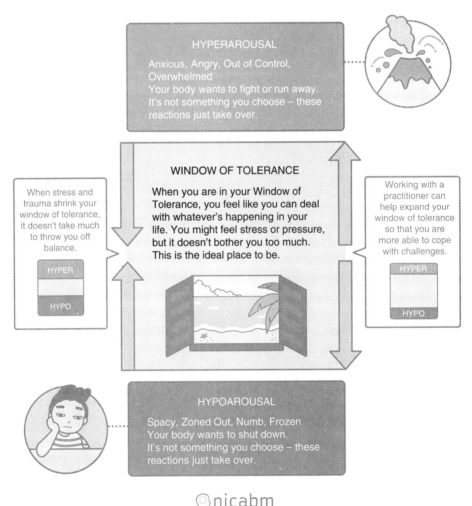

How Trauma Can Affect Your Window of Tolerance

HYPERAROUSAL

Anxious, Angry, Out of Control, Overwhelmed
Your body wants to fight or run away.
It's not something you choose – these reactions just take over.

When stress and trauma shrink your window of tolerance, it doesn't take much to throw you off balance.

HYPER
HYPO

WINDOW OF TOLERANCE

When you are in your Window of Tolerance, you feel like you can deal with whatever's happening in your life. You might feel stress or pressure, but it doesn't bother you too much. This is the ideal place to be.

Working with a practitioner can help expand your window of tolerance so that you are more able to cope with challenges.

HYPER
HYPO

HYPOAROUSAL

Spacy, Zoned Out, Numb, Frozen
Your body wants to shut down.
It's not something you choose – these reactions just take over.

nicabm
www.nicabm.com

© 2023 The National Institute for the Clinical Application of Behavioral Medicine

SOURCE: National Institute for the Clinical Application of Behavioral Medicine https://www.nicabm.com/trauma-how-to-help-your-clients-understand-their-window-of-tolerance/

The Window of Tolerance is when we are at our best, able to cope with the normal levels of stress, anxiety, or trauma we may experience on a daily or weekly basis. It is also the place where our coping skills can be used to keep us within the window. We have restorative relationships with friends and loved ones. We are also using our SEL skills of self-awareness and self-management to be in touch with our mental, emotional, and physical states, and to use positive self-regulation methods to achieve our goals. It's the necessary condition for optimal learning. We also want to keep in mind the context, climate, and environment we are in and how that can support or undermine our window.

When we move out of the Window of Tolerance, we move into a fight–flight–freeze or collapse state of mind. In essence, the amygdala hijacks our logical brain until the prefrontal cortex is engaged so we can problem-solve. Being "hyper"-aroused means feeling anxious, agitated, excited, or angry. On the opposite end of the spectrum, we might be "hypo"-aroused, which is a form of dysregulation when we shut down, freeze up, spacy, or sluggish. Dysregulation occurs when we are experiencing significant symptoms of hyper- or hypoarousal which impacts our capacity and our ability to read the situation. When dysregulated we may be making split decisions that are based less on facts or accurate information. Our brain is primed to jump to conclusions, make faulty assumptions, and respond from a defensive place.

One of the self-reflective skills we can develop is recognizing when we are "out" of the Window of Tolerance. Recognizing when we are triggered provides the opportunity to regulate and bring our nervous system back into balance. The concept of homeostasis is to be able to shift out of defensive states and bring ourselves back into the window of tolerance. We self-regulate constantly throughout the day, often doing it automatically and without knowing it. The problems arise when we are dysregulated and move out of the window rather than in it. Building skills and capacity for self-regulation involves developing tool strategies, practices and strategies that help us to stay in balance.

PAUSE AND REFLECT

Take a moment to think, discuss, or write about these questions:

1. Does your school have a clear definition and understanding of *trauma*? Would you consider your teachers and school to be trauma-informed?

2. Think about the context of your school. What elements of your environment might cause trauma for students and adults?

3. How useful might it be for your students and staff to know about the Window of Tolerance? How might this change what you do in classrooms and your school?

RELATED TIER 2 ISSUES: LONELINESS, ISOLATION, GRIEF, AND LOSS

During the COVID-19 pandemic, it was necessary to isolate ourselves for protection. This meant school-age children spent months apart from each other, leading to isolation and often loneliness. Loneliness and isolation place us in potentially chronic states of stress. Due to the social nature of the brain, we are hardwired for connection. We need relationships to build resiliency, repair damage from stress, and to develop positivity. There is a great deal of difference between being alone and being lonely. Sometimes, we need time alone, especially if we have been around others quite a bit. Some of us are also more introverted and so we relish in those times alone. But being lonely or isolated can bring feelings of sadness, disconnect, or even depression. We might also experience social isolation due to bullying or harassing behaviors of others.

Schools that are oriented toward mental health and flourishing provide opportunities for both social and individual experiences. They understand the negative impact of loneliness and isolation. A school culture that understands the essential nature of relationships and cultivates relationships through cooperative learning, collaborative student and staff spaces, and making time to know each other well will immediately diminish feelings of loneliness and isolation, not only for their students but for their staff and community members.

Another ever-present Tier 2 challenge we all must face at some point is loss and grief. During our lives we lose people we know. For a young person, it might be the death of a grandparent or family friend. And it might be their first experience with loss. For others, we may lose someone quite close to us, a family member, partner, or child. In some instances, the loss may be difficult to understand or process, such as an act of violence, an accident, suicide, or an illness. The context and type of death is an important element in supporting students and staff as it will help guide your response. Grief is a normal part of life. It is a difficult and painful experience. It impacts us physically, emotionally, and socially. Experiences of grief can be life-changing. We need to consider grief, loss and traumatic bereavement in our mental health planning. We also need to consider that in a number of ways we are still impacted by the effects and consequences of the COVID-19 pandemic as it relates to loss and trauma.

In all instances of loss, those who have a relationship with the person who died will experience the stress response and may even be traumatized. Even people with no relationship to the person may have a secondary response to just hearing about the death and it may trigger past experiences or emotions. It is critical for school leaders to understand the many ways that loss can ripple across a school and community. Doing so allows us to build support systems to respond when they occur. It is also important to remember that loss is not just related to death, and that grief can occur with other types of loss.

During a nine-month period in a district we both worked in, the school community suffered through a series of tragedies, including suicide deaths of a staff member, a parent, and a recent graduate. A beloved teacher died unexpectedly from a heart attack. And a current student, his mother, and step-father were killed in a domestic homicide. Thanks to preventative planning years before, the district had a Community Response Network that kept educators, social workers, first responders, and clergy connected and ready at a moment's notice to come to our aid as we dealt with each of these losses. We recognized the importance of communicating information clearly in both private and public ways. We set up opportunities for students, staff, and the community to express their grief and receive support. Our Adviser Room system and the positive relationship between staff and students in classes, clubs, and sports allowed us to process these losses in smaller safe and trusted communities. And we found ways to commemorate these losses weeks and months and even a year later.

With every loss, we also experience grief. Grief is another of those normal human responses, when the emotional center of the brain is triggered. We may be overwhelmed with stress or trauma. It is a difficult and painful experience. Engaging in social and emotional skills at these moments can help, beginning with identifying our own feelings and responses, as well as recognizing that someone else is grieving. Responding to grief and loss begins with relationships for the individual who has experienced loss. It can help to create check-in times with a counselor or trusted adult. A school can also create a group of students who have experienced a loss to come together for mutual support and process their experience together, usually with a trained social worker or counselor leading the group. It is also important to consider providing support for the adults who are working with grieving students. Compassion fatigue is real and our Tier 2 support systems should accommodate it as well. Consider the impact grief has upon all members of the school community.

PAUSE AND REFLECT

Take a moment to think, discuss, or write about these questions:

1. What are some ways you and your staff identify students who are feeling lonely or isolated? How do you connect and support them?

2. What incidents of loss have affected your students, staff, and community?

3. How open are people to discussing loss and the grief they are experiencing?

4. What systems do you have or could you have to facilitate loss and grief?

TIER 2 INTERVENTIONS AND STRATEGIES

The best starting point for designing Tier 2 interventions and support strategies is to recognize the strength of existing Tier 1 interventions and strategies. If the school is employing solid Tier 1 support for all students, there will be a strong foundation upon which to build more specialized Tier 2 strategies. One of those strategies is a culture of caring and relationships that leads to people knowing each other well and noticing when something is not right. It also helps when staff are well trained at noticing things like signs of stress, anxiety, or trauma. The bottom line is that at Tier II we need to NOTICE a potential problem and then INVESTIGATE it to assess the individual and the situation. Let's take a closer look at a variety of Tier 2 interventions and strategies...

Teachers Are the First to Notice

Teachers are often some of the first people to know when a young person is struggling with risky behavior or a mental health issue. This begins with the amount of time they spend with students and the relationship they build with each individual. Teaching is emotional work and teachers are well suited to notice emotional or physical changes, some dysregulation, or cues that something is not right.

Teachers are also connected to parents, family, and caregivers, often seeing them daily or communicating via phone or email. In this way, teachers have an insight into what is happening outside the school environment with a student. This role as teacher and this close relationship is a critical early warning system for potential student problems. Let us add that support staff, coaches, crossing guards, and bus drivers are also essential members of the school staff who build important relationships with kids and notice when things are amiss. That is why school leaders must engage ALL staff in knowing the signs of distress and what to do when they see them.

Knowing the Signs of Distress

The place to start in knowing the signs of distress is understanding how the brain and body respond to stress, anxiety, and trauma. The fight–flight–freeze response or being in a hyperaroused or hypoaroused state of dysregulation results in physiological changes that we can see and verbalizations that we can hear. It also helps if we have baseline data about how a person behaves in a regulated state, when they feel at ease or engaged or "in the flow."

Armed with that information, a teacher, staff member, parent, or fellow student should be able to recognize that something is happening to a student. The time spent building a relationship with another person, often engaged in the kind of learning tasks we do in classrooms and schools, offers us all a great opportunity to get to know a person who is well regulated. Therefore, a culture of collaboration and a focus on relationship-building is foundational for identifying Tier 2 problems in students and adults.

Some of the telltale signs that a student is grappling with mental health issues include the following:

- Feeling very sad or withdrawn for more than two weeks
- Extreme difficulty concentrating or remaining calm
- Drastic mood swings or changes in student behavior
- Sudden overwhelming fear for no reason, sometimes with a racing heart or fast breathing
- Severe out-of-control behavior that can hurt oneself or others
- Changes in diet, either not eating or eating too much
- Repeated use of drugs or alcohol
- Self-harming behaviors or making plans to do so

We also need to learn more about human behavior and how the mind/body/brain work together. Doing so would provide staff with essential knowledge for recognizing when a student is in distress. Schools should invest more time and money into continual professional development about neuroscience, human development, social and emotional learning, stress, anxiety, and trauma. Learning about stress, distress, and the workings of the brain and nervous system can provide a foundation to not only address stress but chronic and toxic stress and trauma. This can also provide a way to address teacher stress and burnout.

Professional development about diversity, equity, and identity is also critical to better knowing students and recognizing the kind of support that will help them as they navigate the intersectionality of identity and basic challenges of mental health. Certainly, classroom teachers will benefit from deeper knowledge on these topics as they develop relationships with their students and get to know them well enough to recognize problems. It will also help them develop more responsive learning environments, lessons, and assessments. As we have noted before, one of the most significant protective factors that school can build is that of relationships, for students to be known and have at least one adult who knows them well.

Beyond PreK–12 schools, teacher preparation programs must do a better job of providing this training to new teachers so they understand from the beginning that these Tier 2 mental health issues are as important as content area knowledge and skills. Support staff such as instructional aides, social workers and counselors, nurses, substitutes, and paraprofessionals, as well as custodial and cafeteria staff, need to have similar training as they interact with students in both formal and informal settings. And, of course, parents and family members should understand these signs so they can respond and report them to educators.

MINDFULNESS IN SCHOOLS

Training students and staff in the art and practice of mindfulness can front-load skills that can support them when they encounter a crisis or feel stress. Mindfulness is a great example of core SEL skills like self-reflection and self-management. It is training your mind to pay attention to what is happening in your mind and body, then using a simple practice like breathing or focus to manage the stress response.

The most basic way to do this is to pause in the moment and take three deep belly breaths. This focuses us on our body, calms the nervous system, and causes our mind to stop what it is doing and pay attention. The more breaths we take, the more we become focused. If we are feeling an emotion, it is also useful to name that emotion aloud or to ourselves. This added step helps us to understand the connection between our mind, body, and emotions.

With young children, teachers and parents will often ask dysregulated students to pause and take three deep breaths or to count to five as a way of calming themselves down. A daily practice of sitting and breathing consciously for thirty seconds or even a minute has been shown to bring calm, focus, and relaxation to a person. Clearly, this simple approach to mindfulness can help when any of us encounter a moment of stress or dysregulation.

Many schools take the concept of mindfulness and weave it into daily classroom and school practices. A school in Chicago has all students and staff start and end their day in a sitting practice to help with the transition into and out of the school day. Many of those teachers also start their class sessions with a short mindfulness activity like journaling or breathing. In another example, an urban college preparatory high school has started "Mindful Mondays," which is a short period every week where students and staff engage in a variety of mindfulness activities, as well as listening to inspirational stories, doing creative activities, and connecting with other students. In one activity, students read Amanda Gorman's inauguration poem "The Hill We Climb" and then watched a video interview where she spoke about her struggles in school to learn and how she overcame them.

The concept of a "Calming Corner" or "Peace Room" has also taken hold in PreK–12 classrooms and schools, which are comfortable spaces where students can choose to use when they need to calm down or manage feelings of stress or anxiety. This could be as simple as a chair, desk, or beanbag chair off to the side with fidget spinners, journal paper, or coloring books. Some schools have an entire room dedicated to mindfulness with comfortable seating, soft lighting, music, and a counselor they can talk to. A school can also provide mindfulness support and activities online, creating a kind of "virtual calm corner" that can be accessed at anytime from anywhere.

CIRCLES

More and more schools are using circles to give students and staff a process for building relationships and safe spaces where people can relax, focus, and be themselves. A circle is a practice with a protocol for a small group of people to communicate. Everyone engaged in the circle agrees to only speak one at a time, with the rest of the group listening and reflecting on what the speaker has said. Usually, a "talking piece" is employed that signifies who is the current speaker. Then the talking piece is passed to the next person who can either hold it and speak or pass it to the next person in the circle. Often, one person in the circle is designated to ask questions or ensure the circle guidelines are followed.

Circles can be used at all three tiers of support we are exploring in this book. In Tier 1, classroom teachers can easily use the circle protocol as a way to lead content discussions. Circles and circle-keeping is very similar to other discussion protocols that language arts and social studies teachers commonly use. Teachers can also use circles to process activities or build community. Athletic coaches and club sponsors have also successfully integrated circles into their team-building and processing activities. Teachers, staff, and administrators are also utilizing circles as a way to talk through issues and connect with each other. One of the strengths of circles is the way it reduces power dynamics between people, especially when they are in roles of authority. Both of us have used circles regularly to start or end meetings, giving everyone a chance to have a voice and to help us transition in and out of a meeting, especially if it has been particularly tense.

In Tier 2, circles can become a powerful go-to strategy for processing crises or repairing a disruption that a community has experienced. Because the protocol itself is grounded in listening and it provides a predictable structure for speaking, circle practices are equitable, safe, and trauma informed. They also can be used in a restorative justice approach to behavior. For example, when a student causes a disruption like making an inappropriate comment or losing control in some way, our traditional response is to focus only on the behavior of the student (often by kicking them out of class) and not on the impact this behavior has on another individual student or the entire class or the teacher. The community has been disrupted. A restorative approach would be to acknowledge what has happened and pull the class or group together into a circle. It gives the student who acted out a chance to explain themselves and apologize, and for the other student or students to express how those actions made them feel. Then the entire group can discuss how to move forward together. Of course, the teacher may need to give the student some kind of consequence, however the focus is to repair the damage they caused, and the circle has provided an opportunity for everyone in the community to process what has happened and to "restore" the community equilibrium.

Additional uses of circles at Tier 2 can address other situations that students and staff experience when it comes to problem-solving or responding to stress or trauma. We have encountered numerous schools that have used circles as a way to process tough topics like racism, immigration, bullying, and politics, sometimes as a way to prepare young people for potential crises or after to process an event. When there has been a death or loss of some kind, circles can provide a structure to process grief both in the short term and long term. A classroom might have a student return from a long absence due to illness, hospitalization, or other circumstance. A circle would be a wonderful way of welcoming that student back into the community. And we can also use circles to celebrate positive events or experiences. These can be as powerful as the other types of circles we've discussed.

While we will explore Tier 3 in more depth in the next chapter, it is a good time for us to look at how circles can be used with more serious issues facing students and staff. In instances where serious harm or disruption has occurred and some manner of restorative discipline has been instituted, a circle can be a powerful way of repairing the harm and rebuilding connection and community among and between students. These kinds of healing circles or repairing harm circles often require an experienced facilitator who can ask good questions and manage the circle process, especially if emotions are high. Conflict resolution is one of the best times to use a circle practice, even with a small group of students or adults because the power differential between people and roles is equalized, providing space for a person's voice to be heard safely and hopefully received deeply. Both of these are essential in working through a conflict or healing after one.

Circles have ancient roots and modern branches. By design they are focused upon being inclusive and a place where everyone is welcome and everyone helps to find solutions. Circles can build community by teaching how to be "in community." They are powerful by creating a space where everyone has the opportunity to speak and be heard, where no one is left out. Circles build relational trust. It's an interactive form where all voices are honored and where the person as an individual is valued. The circle process is a storytelling process, recognizing that every person has a story and every story has a lesson to offer. It's a process and technique for ongoing effective group communication, relationship-building, decision-making, conflict mediation, and resolution. It's a safe space physically and psychologically.

Kay Pranis is a leading expert on the use of circles in schools and organizations. Her book *Circle Forward* (Boyes-Watson & Pranis, 2020) describes in detail how circles can be applied in a number of different situations and how to lead groups in circle practices. Recently, Pranis described the connection between mindfulness and circles: "The partnership between circles and mindfulness has the potential to transform the emotional landscape of a school without adding any personnel. Both techniques are highly accessible and highly adaptable. Students can be taught to use circles and mindfulness techniques without depending on an adult to initiate or lead the process." In Figure 4.1, Pranis provides an MTSS framework for circles and examples of specific tier-based practices.

FIGURE 4.1 CIRCLE PRACTICE TIER STRUCTURE: MINDSET OF EACH LEVEL, GOALS OF EACH LEVEL, PRACTICES OF EACH LEVEL

Tier 1: Building Healthy Community	
Mindset	• Healthy community is essential for effective learning because healthy community creates emotional and physical safety and frees the brain for higher functions. • Healthy community requires a positive sense of belonging for every member of the community. • Attention to building healthy community is required for every part of the community: students, noncertified staff, certified staff, parents, support services (e.g., buses) . . . • Circle practice is an excellent tool for practicing the skills of being in healthy community. • Building and maintaining healthy community requires on-going attention and commitment. • Healthy community promotes better learning outcomes.
Goals	• Increase sense of belonging, emotional intelligence, mutual respect, collective responsibility of all sectors of the community. • Practice the skills required for a healthy community in a non-stressful context. • Create joy in connection.
Practices	• Celebration circles • Check-in circles • Learning circles • Community building circles • Mindfulness

Continued

Tier 2: Repairing Disruptions to Community	
Mindset	• Disruptions in relationships are a normal part of the human experience. • Disruptions in community relationships undermine the health of the community and therefore the learning environment. • A healing response to the disruption can reestablish healthy community relationships and a sense of belonging and safety in the community to facilitate a focus on learning. • Circle practice can be an excellent tool for reestablishing healthy community relationships after a disruption.
Goals	• Create a space to acknowledge the disruption and its impact on members of the community. • Engage community support for one another in working through the impact of the disruption. • Reinforce the sense of belonging for everyone as the basis of healthy community. • Engage genuine accountability where that is a factor in the disruption. • Identify steps to prevent a similar disruption in the future if that is relevant. • Create a sense of hope and optimism for moving forward in a constructive way from the disruption.
Practices	• Transition circles • Collective problem-solving circles • Healing circles for individual impact • Grief and loss circles for collective impact • Conflict circles for less serious conflicts • Harm circles for less serious harms
Tier 3: Rebuilding Serious Disruptions to Community	
Mindset	• Serious disruptions to the community fabric reduce learning opportunities. • Serious disruptions to the community fabric may indicate a lack of healthy community from the beginning—a failure of the community to create a sense of belonging or respect for every member. • Serious disruptions to the community fabric require intensive rebuilding of relationships. • High levels of distrust of the community take time to heal. • Complex factors may contribute to serious disruptions of community connection and consequently solutions may require engagement of partners outside of the school. • Circles are an excellent tool for understanding complexity of causes and for revealing chronic conditions contributing to the disruption and for creating long term solutions that improve the learning environment for all students.
Goals	• Create healing spaces for identified harms (caused by or revealed by the situation). • Engage all stakeholders in crafting a long-term solution to harms and causes of the disruption. • Rebuild or build for the first time a sense of belonging and worth for everyone involved or impacted by the situation. • Leave the community stronger than it was before the disruption happened or was identified.

Continued

FIGURE 4.1 CIRCLE PRACTICE TIER STRUCTURE: MINDSET OF EACH LEVEL, GOALS OF EACH LEVEL, PRACTICES OF EACH LEVEL *(CONTINUED)*

Practices	• Healing circles • Conflict circles for serious or chronic conflicts • Harm circles for serious or chronic harms • Support circles for anyone needing on-going support to heal or to change life patterns • Community circles to examine underlying causes and community accountability

SOURCE: Adapted from Kay Pranis (2019).

PAUSE AND REFLECT

Take a moment to think, discuss, or write about these questions:

1. How would your school define *mindfulness*?

2. What mindfulness activities are being used in your school right now?

3. How could they be used in your school?

4. What has your experience been with circles? How might they be useful in your school?

STUDENT BEHAVIOR AND DISCIPLINE: A SHIFT TO RESTORATIVE PRACTICES

Behavior is a form of communication. Misbehaviors are usually the result of unmet needs or underdeveloped skills. In a 2023 survey of teachers, almost 70% said student behavior was worse than it was two years ago, a statistic that has not changed much in a decade (Prothero, 2023). Student behavior and consequential disciplinary action is a major topic of both preservice teacher training and veteran teacher conversations. Some school administrators do nothing but manage student behavior and discipline every single day! The definition of this Tier 2 issue usually includes moments when an individual student becomes dysregulated or decides to break a classroom or school rule. Entire student handbooks exist that delineate what is expected and what is discouraged, as well as important due process rights and procedures. We encourage you to take a deep dive into not only your printed procedures regarding student behavior but also the unwritten culture and history at your particular school. This should be a starting point for any comprehensive Mental Health Action Plan.

We have already alluded to a difference between traditional behavior management philosophies and others that might be more in line with supporting student mental health (see Figure 4.2). Traditionally, schools have employed a disciplinary or punitive model for behavior, which is reactive, consequence driven, compliance oriented, and focused on individual behavior, power, and control. In contrast, many schools and states are moving to a restorative practice model, which is proactive, reflective, collaborative, solution oriented, with a focus on problem-solving and community-building. Instead of excluding students for misbehavior, we find ways of keeping them and reintegrating them into the community, as we described in the section on Circles earlier.

Unfortunately, most teachers, administrators, and parents can only imagine a traditional, punitive approach since that is what most of them experienced, both as students and as adults, so the shift to a restorative approach is a shift in both mindset and skillset.

FIGURE 4.2 DIFFERENCE BETWEEN TRADITIONAL BEHAVIOR MODELS AND RESTORATIVE MODELS

TRADITIONAL MODEL	RESTORATIVE MODEL
Reactive	Reflective, proactive
Consequence	Solution focus, problem-solving
Focus on individual behavior	Building community, reintegrating
Power and control	Relationship-building
Compliance oriented	Collaborative

Restorative practices are focused upon the repair of harm that may have been caused. They range from incidents in which there's a teachable moment in the classroom. Restorative practices in school are based upon restoring positive relationships. Rather than focusing upon the violation of rules, it's a process in which dialog occurs and the people involved are allowed to explore the behavior and the context and come to an understanding of why the behavior occurred and what can be done positively to repair and set things right. It's a problem solving process in which everyone involved has an opportunity to more fully understand what has happened, who has been affected, what can be done to repair the harm, and to prevent similar situations from happening in the future.

Restorative practices and restorative discipline are rooted in the foundational assumption that everyone wants to be in a good relationship, and that everybody wants to be respected and treated with care and dignity. A physically and psychologically safe environment aligns policies, procedures, and programs that enhance school climate, builds community, relationships, and capacity for problem-solving. It embeds restorative practices like circle-keeping, specifically a circle of care, through each tier of the MTSS model. Kay Pranis says, "everything experienced in circle contributes to building community and trauma healing ... every time we are in circle, we're teaching SEL."

We strongly encourage school leaders and teachers to think about how circles, especially circles of care, can be used on a daily basis in the school to provide capacity to integrate and manage stress, for belonging and connection through storytelling, to prepare students to understand each other, and to repair and heal when harm is done. Circles build accountability, responsibility, and community. They are a powerful tool in a restorative approach to behavior.

As you take a closer look at your philosophy on student behavior and the response systems that have been created, be wary of zero-tolerance policies. Zero-tolerance approaches rely heavily upon detention, suspensions, and expulsions to manage student behavior. Study after study shows that zero-tolerance policies do not deter negative behaviors but rather increase the school to prison pipeline that has developed over the past 50 years (Camera, 2021). Shifting a focus away from coercion and use of punishment and rewards to achieve compliance is a shift toward the quality of relationships between teacher and students, and students and each other. These relationships are based upon trust, caring, and a sense of belonging. Except in the most extreme situations involving weapons or criminal behavior, a zero-tolerance policy should not be a part of a comprehensive Mental Health Action Plan.

As for suspensions, consider alternatives to suspensions that pair students with adult mentors or use student groups that address risk behavior and teach coping strategies. Include parents at every step to create alignment between what is happening in school with what is happening at home. The more we can due to keep students IN school, the better chance we have of breaking the school-to-prison pipeline.

Traditionally, schools have taken a consequential, reactive, punitive stance toward discipline and behavior. We need to consider that when "mis"-behavior occurs, it often is done because of a need that has not been met, a skill that has not been developed, or a condition that needs to be addressed. Schools need to consider how restorative practices can be used instead of punitive discipline to improve and address mental health. This needs to be done throughout a school system so that everyone has shifted to a more restorative mindset.

PAUSE AND REFLECT

Take a moment to think, discuss, or write about these questions:

1. Would you consider your school's approach to behavior to be rooted in a traditional model or a restorative model?

2. When was the last time your student handbook was deeply reviewed by all stakeholders?

3. Do you have zero-tolerance policies in your handbook?

4. What restorative practices do you already have integrated in your school?

TRAUMA-INFORMED PRACTICE

Trauma-informed care focuses upon safety and support. It seeks to create an environment that is safe, secure, and resourced enough for all students and staff. Where there are positive relationships and easy access to mental health support. Where self-care practices are woven into the culture through predictable routines, strong relationships, and the development of SEL skills, executive functioning, and self-regulation. Where policies and practices align to support mental health and build community. The CDC's Office of Readiness and Response (2020) and SAMHSA's National Center for Trauma-Informed Care (2023) have identified six principles that should guide trauma-informed care:

1. Safety

2. Trustworthiness and transparency

3. Peer support

4. Collaboration and mutuality

5. Empowerment and choice

6. Cultural, historical and gender issues

Recently, educators, students, families, and community members have started to demand that everything we do in schools should be trauma informed. This is a recognition of both the scope and impact trauma has on learning and development. A Tier 2 response to either previous or current trauma is to create classrooms and schools that understand the psychological and physical impact of trauma on young people. A scan of the school would identify those things that might trigger a response from a traumatized student, such as loud music or noise in the hallway or a classroom. Some schools have put diffusers on lights to reduce the harsh light emanating from fluorescent bulbs. Teachers analyze their practice in classrooms to create a calm yet engaging climate where students can feel comfortable taking risks academically. Student behavior responses change from "What's wrong with you?" to "What has/is happening to you?" "What are your strengths? What resources/support do you need?"

A trauma-informed school also emphasizes those things that can restore harm from trauma and build resilience in students, things like self-reflection, authentic relationships, cooperative learning, altruism and community service, and self-care. While some of these should be part of Tier 1 support for all students, there are moments when individual students will need additional support when they are managing the outcomes of past or current trauma.

Trauma-informed approaches are also practices that emphasize self-care for staff. A critical aspect of Tier 2 interventions is to recognize the impact that stress, crisis and trauma have upon the day-to-day lives of teachers in the classroom, something called *secondary trauma*, the empathic strain, the wear and tear of experiences that impact teacher or staff emotional health and well-being. Due to the empathetic nature of teaching, there is always a concern about burnout. But when students are managing crisis and trauma the impact on teachers, staff, and administrators can be huge. Schools must provide resources throughout the organization that can support teachers not only in the joy of teaching but also opportunities for growth, support, and healing.

Trauma is always in the room and present. We need to have a foundational, conceptual understanding of what trauma is and its impact. We need a trauma lens, as well as practices that help and don't harm. Trauma-informed practices are built upon priorities of safety and emphasize a holistic, whole-child approach that is integrated with a focus on the developmental, social, emotional, physiological, and mental health of all. If we look at behaviors without considering the complex and lasting impact of trauma, schools run the risk of retraumatizing students. Every adult in the building should be trained in understanding trauma and be SEL trauma informed. Every school should have integrated policies, language, and practices that not only support students but also staff, that support teachers and staff in their mental health.

SMALL GROUPS

A powerful Tier 2 intervention is providing opportunities for students to collaborate around a common issue or problem. Usually, a trained adult staff member or community member acts as the facilitator and the specific topic could be based on needs that have arisen within individual students or portions of the student population, were identified on school climate or other surveys, or were suggested by students themselves. The goal is to give students a safe place to work with and support each other, possibly building specific skills that will help them manage the problem or issue facing them. Some potential topics for student small groups include:

- Stress management
- Anger management
- Communication skills
- Conflict mediation
- Race, class, gender affinity groups
- Transition groups for incoming students
- Students returning from hospitalization
- Grief/Loss group
- Bullying and harassment
- Problem-solving and decision-making

Small groups at Tier 2 can address early intervention and risk behaviors that may range from addressing anxiety to preventing high risk behaviors like drug and alcohol use, abuse, or bullying behavior. There are a variety of group intervention models that include behavior management, Cognitive Behavioral Intervention for Trauma in Schools (CBITS), and Dialectical Behavior Therapy (DBT). In addition, there are alternative therapeutic interventions that may include dance movement, expressive arts music, and experiential therapy.

In one school, the social workers created a small group called Mangoes, named by students, to support the social and emotional needs of students who experienced a significant loss such as the death of a family member or significant person in their lives. This open-ended small group was designed to be a safe and secure environment in which students could share their experience, their feelings, and the impact the loss may be having in their lives and particularly in school. By providing a supportive network of peers who understand the experiences and challenges of loss, staff were there to engage and respond to their social emotional needs, enhance healing, and reduce vulnerability. The emotional support of a regular weekly loss group where students can share their experience and tell their stories can facilitate the adjustment to loss and enhance the ability to cope with the many demands of a life-changing experience of loss.

PEER HELPING, MEDIATION, MENTORING, AND TUTORING

One of the great untapped resources in our schools are the students themselves. There are many instances when students can be positioned to help each other, especially when they are dealing with a temporary challenge. A peer-mentoring program pairs two students together, one who is usually more experienced than the other, and provides them with space and time to support the new student. Many schools have leveraged students to work with each other to mediate conflict or provide support. These activities and groups should be supervised by a teacher or staff member but the goal is to get kids helping other kids.

In one K–12 school, older students are trained in skills and supervised to help mediate disputes between students at younger grades. Student mediators are trained by staff on protocols for creating safe spaces where two students can talk through a dispute and come to some equitable outcome. Some schools offer students a choice of working through a problem with an administrator or going to peer mediation or peer jury. Students agreeing to work with a peer mediator can feel that they are treated more fairly by another student, and the peer mediators learn valuable skills on how to talk with others and navigate difficult situations.

Another school we have worked with has a cadre of students engaged in what they call "Peer Helping." This voluntary group of high school students meet several days a week during their lunch periods to develop skills, build community, and to organize programs that benefit all students. Each year, the group and their faculty sponsor survey the students on what issues are important to them. Then, they develop a year-long plan of activities to address the issues raised. Some topics seem to come up year after year, such as an annual blood drive, health fair, and new-student orientation. One year, the group identified sexual assault as an important topic and organized a series of workshops for students to learn about it, including bring the Clothesline Project to the high school, which is a national program in which victims and survivors or assault share their stories and experiences through visual designs on T-shirts. Health classes and Advisories would visit the display and then have discussions afterward that were moderated by peer helpers.

Academically, one of the best ways to engage students in addressing Tier 2 issues is through peer tutoring. Once again, tutors are selected, trained, and supported by adult staff members. It is very important for them to not only know the content well but also different strategies for helping students who might be struggling or need a particular approach. It is also important to dedicate comfortable and supervised space for students to work with each other.

Peer tutors can be generalists, helping with several content areas but also supporting study strategies, time management, or test-taking. They can also be specific to focus on content areas such as math, writing, science, or world languages. Peer-tutoring programs not only help students academically, but they also create a culture of caring between students while providing valuable leadership skill training for tutors. It also provides teachers with an added layer of academic support they can offer students.

PAUSE AND REFLECT

Take a moment to think, discuss, or write about these questions:

1. What are some ways your school provides opportunities for students to help each other?

2. What training do you provide staff who led these kinds of student-focused groups?

3. What role do students play in conflict resolution and role-modeling?

ANTI-BULLYING PROGRAMS

As we have seen, young people need to be explicitly taught social skills. This is especially true in relationship-based schools. A strong anti-bullying curriculum and programming can be incredibly helpful in developing a caring community from preschool and kindergarten up through high school. As a Tier 1 prevention strategy, schools can teach students about the power dynamics that can exist in certain relationships and how to identify when someone is using bullying behavior, what it looks like to be a bystander, as well as how to be an ally. Common language can be taught and used across the school by students and staff to describe these actions and how to respond to them.

Many elementary schools have identified benches on playgrounds as "Buddy Benches" where a student can go if they want to indicate they are looking for someone to play with. Middle school and high school Advisories can be places to process peer pressure and bullying situations, then role-play how to work through them. This is another great reason to use circles and circle-keeping in schools so the entire class, team, or club can have a safe place to work through a bullying situation. Student, Staff, and Parent/Family Handbooks should indicate that bullying and harassing behaviors are not tolerated here, along with the process used to negotiate those situations.

There are some wonderful anti-bullying programs and curricula that schools can use to make anti-bullying a centerpiece of their school. These can not only serve as a Tier 1 prevention strategy but also provide essential Tier 2 support when bullying needs to be targeted for intervention, often in middle school or early high school. The Anti-Defamation League provides educators with training and materials through "A World of Difference" and "Becoming an Ally." Both dive into diversity, intergroup relations, bias, bullying, harassment, bystanding, and allyship. The Second Step social and emotional learning curriculum includes a bullying prevention unit for Grades K–5 that provides younger students with the skills and practice on how to recognize, report, and prevent bullying behaviors.

One high school we both worked with created their own Bullying and Harassment Action Committee, made up of students, staff, and parents, as a way to develop their own custom programs that responded to the unique issues facing their school and community. Students wrote skits and made videos that could be shared widely through health and physical education classes, as well as Advisories. Student leaders facilitated circle conversations with their peers to identify ways of avoiding bullying behaviors and how to become an ally.

The committee also discussed the question of how school culture defines *adult behavior* in a way that interferes with professionalism and promotes bullying, harassment, and bystanding. What is privileged and honored and what is not? They explored hierarchy and power dynamics based on roles, competitiveness, miscommunication, and structural barriers to bringing people together. These kinds of collaborative efforts can occur across PreK–12 and go a long way in preventing and responding to bullying and harassment.

STUDENT ACTIVITIES AND CLUBS

Schools should recognize the important role student clubs and activities play in supporting positive mental health, especially as Tier 2 interventions for students with specific interests. As a Tier 1 prevention system, a healthy student activities and athletics program provide students with social connection, opportunities to learn new skills, and bodily-kinesthetic activities. For some students, these are the very reasons they get out of bed every day to come to school!

Student clubs and athletic teams can also be important spaces for students to get peer support during moments of stress, anxiety, or dysregulation, especially if they are connected to something they are passionate about. For example, an English teacher who sponsors an after-school poetry slam club gives students a chance to explore their experiences growing up through creative expression and receive support from other members of the club.

These activities can become part of a broader mission to improve mental health across the entire school. We've already explored how peer helping, mentoring, and tutoring can provide those involved with a sense of altruism while also helping others. The same can be true for student clubs focused on issues like physical health, mental health, mindfulness, yoga, equity, environmentalism, healthy eating, student rights, and student government. Affinity groups are also powerful activities that bring students together around race, class, gender, and ability, giving them opportunities to meet over common interests and background, and also providing space to explore ways of sharing their points of view with the entire school community. Several schools we have worked with have seen students find connection through groups like a Black Student Union, LatinX Club, Asian-American Club, and LGBTQ Allies.

PAUSE AND REFLECT

Take a moment to think, discuss, or write about these questions:

1. What is your approach to teaching anti-bullying skills and knowledge?

2. Does your school offer clubs, affinity groups, and activities that are of real interest to students?

3. Do you see clubs and activities as a place to teach SEL skills and provide mental health support?

PARENT/FAMILY EDUCATION, PROGRAMS, AND ENGAGEMENT

One of the best investments of time (and very little money) a school can make is providing continuing education and learning for parents and families. So many of our parents are first-time parents, navigating both child-rearing and schooling. They are hungry for information, advice, and guidance about parenting, child development, and challenges to learning. Many schools and districts provide workshops, speakers, panel discussions, book groups, and reading material, creating a kind of "Parent University" where these issues can be explored and questions can be asked. This also puts educators and administrators in direct contact with parents and allows them to align the school's goals with those of parents. Their current school probably does things differently than the schools they attended as children! Parent and family education programs help get everyone on the same page so students can be supported in and out of school.

We were very fortunate to have an active and engaged parent and family community at our school. This started with the Parent's Association, which had grade-level representatives who not only supported Advisories and homerooms but they also provided valuable orientation to new parents and learning to all parents and families. The leadership of this association had close contact with the principal and other administrators, which resulted in many opportunities for coordination and a feedback loop between the school and parents.

The other strong organization in the community was the "Family Action Network" or FAN, which started as a drug and alcohol education program but grew into a parent and family education organization that brought in child development and education experts and authors to speak with hundreds of parents, families, educators, and community members every month (Family Action Network, 2023). Over time, their scope grew to include positive psychology, technology, creative arts, and relationships. Today, this organization offers both in-person and online speakers that reach thousands of people both locally and nationally and has included such experts as Howard Gardner, Carol Dweck, Bryan Stephenson, Brene Brown, Ta-Nehesi Coates, Temple Grandin, Ibram Kendi, Daniel Pink, and the late Representative John Lewis. Partnering with parents groups and community organizations can be a powerful way to extend learning to your families and parents and community.

A HEALTHY AND WELL-REGULATED STAFF

A dysregulated teacher cannot help a dysregulated child. At the same time, a healthy, regulated teacher has a much better chance of helping a dysregulated child. In so many ways, the greatest resource for preventing and intervening Tier 2 challenges such as stress, anxiety, and trauma are the adults who work in the school. Therefore, it is imperative that schools do whatever they can to provide the conditions and support for teachers and staff to not only "do their jobs" but to be healthy both physically and mentally.

We have learned many valuable lessons from the COVID-19 pandemic. One is that teachers and staff must be resourced enough and given ample mental and physical health support. Another is that we cannot expect that teacher self-care alone is enough. Yes, we absolutely advocate that teachers should be reflecting deeply on their own self-care and wellness. However, we cannot believe that they can do this all by themselves. It is critical that administrators and school boards provide resources, time, space, and funds to create healthy, safe working conditions in schools so teachers and staff can do their jobs at the highest level.

Teachers, administrators, and staff should engage in regular self-reflection on their own resiliency, coping skills, social and emotional skills, and physical wellness. Just like physical, personal hygiene, every adult should have a "Mental Health Hygiene Plan" they attend to every day that revitalizes them, creates space for self-reflection, connects them with colleagues, family, and friends, provides for healthy food, sleep, and exercise, and provides balance to the emotional drain of caring for young people. They should constantly be learning about the things that challenge our wellness like stress, anxiety, and trauma, as well as the activities that re-fill our buckets and allow us to cope with the normal challenges of being an educator.

School leaders can play a pivotal role in creating a school culture that supports the health and wellness of teachers and staff. As we have already discussed, professional development and learning about all aspects of mental and physical health should be a standard part of every school year. Healthy food, clean drinking water, and spaces for physical activity and exercise need to be available to every adult in the building. Some schools have dedicated space for staff wellness rooms, while others offer different food options for the adults that might be more appropriate for an adult's palette. A self-care guide for teachers can provide valuable tips and suggestions, as well as signaling that wellness is important here.

Two of the most effective ways schools can improve the mental health of teachers is time and coaching. While some of our time in schools is dictated by the needs of our students, that should be balanced with the needs of our adults. School schedules should be created in ways that prioritize planning time, eating, rest, and collaboration. Many teachers note that job embedded professional development that is baked into the daily and yearly schedule is the best way for them to continue growing and revitalizing themselves.

Connected to this is a commitment in the school to collaboration, coaching, and mentoring. New teachers need additional support and advice in their first few years. That goes for new leaders and administrators! Instructional coaching is quickly becoming an essential part of being a professional educator as teachers support teachers. To combat isolation, all staff should be encouraged to find a "thought partner" or "breakfast buddy" they can meet with occasionally, discuss ideas, and support each other. Seasoned leaders also need support and the resources to meet the challenges of leadership and stress.

Take a moment to think, discuss, or write about these questions:

1. In what ways do you provide your parents and families with support and learning about child development, social and emotional learning, neuroscience, and content learning?

2. In what ways does your school provide mental and physical wellness to staff? How does your school culture support the wellness of all adults?

FINAL THOUGHTS

These are just some of the Tier 2 possibilities you can include in your comprehensive Mental Health Action Plan. Each school should do a needs analysis of what challenges students and staff face in their own context and design intervention strategies to support them when they need it the most. This should start with a solid Tier 1 system of support for all students and staff, then build systems that support moments of higher than normal stress, anxiety, trauma, or crisis. It is not a matter if but when each of us will need this kind of extra support. By planning for the most common challenges, we will be ready. And we will have the capacity to be creative when unforeseen challenges arise. Tier 1 and Tier 2 prevention and intervention strategies form the biggest part of a Mental Health Action Plan. As we will see in the next chapter, they also provide an essential foundation for supporting the most challenging issues in Tier 3.

CREATING YOUR MENTAL HEALTH ACTION PLAN

Take some time to work with your school-based team to think through the following elements of your comprehensive Mental Health Action Plan. The full plan template is located in Appendix A.

Prevention and Intervention Plan: Tier 2

1. What programs or resources do we have that address the following?

   - Stress _____

   - Emotion _____

   - Anxiety _____

   - Crisis and Trauma _____

   - Grief and Loss _____

   - Transitions _____

2. How do we know a student is struggling in or out of school? What are the signs?

   _____

3. What staff development programs do we have to ensure that staff know how to recognize early signs and symptoms of mental health concerns?

   _____

4. How do we screen for early identification of potential problems and student concerns?

   _____

5. What are some interventions we can try to support people who are struggling?

```



```

6. How and where are we teaching coping, resiliency, and trauma response?

```



```

7. How do we provide resources that support staff and teacher wellness? What policies or practices do we have in our staff handbook that address mental health and well-being?

```



```

8. Do we engage and include students as leaders, problem-solvers, and decision-makers in the process of addressing mental health?

```



```

9. What community partnerships do we have in place with organizations and institutions? What's the referral process and procedure?

```



```

10. How do we support parents in their development?

```



```

11. How do we define *trauma-informed practice*?

```



```

REFERENCES

American Psychological Association. (2022). *Stress in America 2022: Concerned for the future, beset by inflation.* https://www.apa.org/news/press/releases/stress/2022/concerned-future-inflation

Bethune, S. (2014, April 1). Teen stress rivals that of adults. *Monitor on Psychology, 45*(4). https://www.apa.org/monitor/2014/04/teen-stress

Boyes-Watson, C., & Pranis, K. (2020). *Circle forward: Building a restorative school community.* Living Justice Press.

Camera, L. (2021, July 27). *Study confirms school-to-prison pipeline.* U.S. News and World Report. https://www.usnews.com/news/education-news/articles/2021-07-27/study-confirms-school-to-prison-pipeline

Centers for Disease Control and Prevention. *Youth Risk Behavior Surveillance System.* https://www.cdc.gov/healthyyouth/data/yrbs/index.htm

Centers for Disease Control and Prevention. (2020). *6 guiding principles to a trauma-informed approach.* https://www.cdc.gov/orr/infographics/6_principles_trauma_info.htm

Centers for Disease Control and Prevention. (2023). *Data and statistics on children's mental health.* https://www.cdc.gov/childrensmentalhealth/data.html

Family Action Network. (2023). www.familyactionnetwork.net

National Institute for the Clinical Application of Behavioral Medicine. (2023). *How to help your clients understand their window of tolerance.* https://www.nicabm.com/trauma-how-to-help-your-clients-understand-their-window-of-tolerance/

Prothero, A. (2023, April 20). Student behavior isn't getting any better, survey shows. *EducationWeek.* https://www.edweek.org/leadership/student-behavior-isnt-getting-any-better-survey-shows/2023/04

Schaefer, N., Rotermund, C., Blumrich, E. M., Lourenco, M. V., Joshi, P., Hegemann, R. U., Jamwal, S., Ali, N., García Romero, E. M., Sharma, S., Ghosh, S., Sinha, J. K., Loke, H., Jain, V., Lepeta, K., Salamian, A., Sharma, M., Golpich, M., Nawrotek, K., . . . Turner, A. J. (2017). The malleable brain: Plasticity of neural circuits and behavior—A review from students to students. *Journal of Neurochemistry, 142*(6), 790–811.

Siegel, D. (1999). *The developing mind.* Guilford Press.

Substance Abuse and Mental Health Services Administration. (2014). *SAMHSA's concept of trauma and guidance for a trauma-informed approach.* HHS Publication No. (SMA) 14-4884. Author.

Substance Abuse and Mental Health Services Administration. (2023). U.S. Department of Health and Human Services. www.samhsa.gov

CHAPTER 5

· ·

TIER 3: SUPPORTING STUDENTS AND STAFF WITH THE GREATEST NEEDS

Trauma is not just a mental health problem. It is an educational problem that, left unaddressed, derails the academic achievement of thousands of children.

> —Susan E. Craig, Trauma Sensitive Schools: Learning Communities Transforming Children's Lives

Sammy is a fourteen-year-old Caucasian male, a ninth grader who is disengaged, defiant, and disruptive in school. Sammy has dark features—short brown hair, brown eyes, dark clothes. Over the course of the past few weeks, he has changed his hair color multiple times. He is dressed in baggy clothes that are oversized, usually with T-shirts for alternative or heavy metal rock bands and high-top sneakers. He maintains regular eye contact, but his eyes frequently wander the room during conversation. The tone of his voice is usually moderate, except when he is excited; during those times, the volume and pitch intensify.

The dean of students at the high school met with Sammy multiple times in just the first few weeks of the school year due to incidents both in and out of the classroom. The dean has tried a variety of responses that have included lunch detentions, suspensions, parent conferences, referral to the Student Support Team and social worker, an alternative to suspension group, and a peer mentor. None of which seem to help. The Student Support Team has asked one of the school social workers to do a case study on Sammy's situation.

(Continued)

(Continued)

She finds that Sammy is a chronically depressed adolescent boy who experienced early and serious sexual trauma, intense parental conflict (which subsequently resulted in divorce), and inconsistent parenting that was detached, aloof, and erratic. He is the older of two siblings. Although he lives with his mother and brother, he has regular weekly contact with his father. His relationship with his mother can be characterized as hostile-dependent, and with father as compliant, passive, and guarded. Sammy was referred to a community-based therapist to work with him and his mother. An additional behavioral concern is his penchant for being triggered and angry which then results in violence. In one example, he took a baseball bat and was beating upon his mother's bedroom door. He also struggles with truancy and drug use, once being caught using marijuana at school. Teachers are concerned about him. They describe him as a bright, engageable, and insightful adolescent boy. He has many strengths, with a wide range of interests and a broad spectrum of friends.

Sammy's story is not uncommon. Every day, some of our students are struggling against an array of issues, some in their control but many that are not. As educators, our purpose is to help students learn and grow. We use every resource at our disposal to create the best learning environment for each individual and to support them on their journey. But when they struggle, we must move away from asking "What is wrong with you?" and instead ask "What is happening to you?" When we make this subtle but powerful shift, we start to use different methods to truly support the student's needs rather than those of the school or the staff.

In this chapter, we will delve into the most difficult challenges facing schools, administrators, and teachers in today's schools. You will learn more about mental illness, including childhood trauma, Adverse Childhood Experiences (ACEs), substance use, eating disorders, nonsuicidal self-injury, depression, suicidal ideation, and suicide. We'll also revisit the issue of equity, as well as the concept of comorbidity and how several of these mental health challenges can impact individuals at the same time. Then we'll turn to what some schools are doing to intervene and support students and adults struggling with these issues. We'll also offer examples of programs, organizations, and resources you can turn to as you build your Mental Health Action Plan.

DEFINING TIER 3 AND HOW IT CONNECTS TO TIERS 1 AND 2

Sometimes we encounter a challenge that can't easily be fixed by Tier 1 or Tier 2 interventions. The students at Tier 3 are the 1% to 5% of students in our schools who are experiencing serious problems and are at risk of developing even more complicated issues. Tier 3 interventions require additional layers of intensive support. This support is usually highly specialized and requires specific training. For most teachers and school leaders, this means recognizing the signs of serious problems and then bringing in a specialist to work directly with the student. It means understanding trauma and traumatic stress, then integrating trauma-informed principles, practices, and policies.

Interventions targeting high-risk students must always take into account stress and stressors such as racism, sexism, classism, poverty, family risk factors such as separation or divorce, trauma, abuse, substance use, and domestic or community violence. These may include serious illnesses, loss, and significant separations or transitions. Consider the impact and the cumulative effect of risk factors such as these and how they impact student adjustment. Mental health problems occur when we're forced to deal with stressors that exceed our capacity to cope. They affect and impact our everyday functioning. They impact not only the individual but can have a rippling effect on the school.

A mental health problem is different and distinct from a mental illness. A mental illness is a medical condition that affects the mind, body and brain. Underlying mental illness may result or be seen as depression, anxiety disorders, post-traumatic stress disorder, substance abuse, self-injury, suicidal ideation, and suicide. They may be evident as behavioral, emotional, or regulation difficulties or neural developmental difficulties; a comprehensive multifaceted understanding provides a framework that allows for interventions that strengthen and support a student's ability to stabilize and engage in learning.

As always, the interventions we design and use with the more complex challenges to mental health rest upon the universal and specialized interventions we have implemented for all students in Tier 1 and Tier 2. In Tier 1, we use universal strategies that are focused upon education and prevention-oriented activities. In the early interventions, we looked at the basics of stress, coping strategies, brain functioning, and SEL skills. Tier 1 interventions are universal supports that build skills, strength, and capacities that promote good mental health. Schools should have a common language around SEL, opportunities to learn and practice those skills throughout the curriculum, and integrate them into every classroom every day. The school is a safe haven, a climate and culture that promotes health for all.

Targeted interventions in Tier 2 reduce stress, anxiety, and trauma throughout the school, and try to teach coping skills and deepen relationships between students, staff, and families. Early identification of student struggles through morning meetings, advisories, or simple screeners can provide an intervention sooner and get the student back on track. Behavior and discipline systems should be oriented toward restorative justice and learning rather than being punitive. Support systems should be integrated and aligned with each other so interventions such as peer support, student groups, and circles can be used at all levels and both staff and parents are on the same page.

Tier 3 interventions are more intense, may need to be offered for a longer duration, and are focused upon stabilization. Interventions require more collaboration and a team-oriented approach that monitors progress, fosters communication, and provides appropriate support. Since the problems are more complicated, the assessment of the situation requires a much more nuanced approach, usually involving a case study that is a detailed description of what is happening and the context. It is critical to understand the meaning behind a behavior, instead of just focusing on the behavior itself. Finally, there is a good chance that the major problem that brings the student to the attention of the staff is not the only issue. Comorbidity of issues such as mental illness, substance abuse, or trauma means support will need to be tailored to each of these other issues.

DEFINING MENTAL ILLNESS

Let's begin our exploration of Tier 3 issues and support by first understanding mental illness. *Mental illness* is defined by the National Association of Mental Illness (NAMI, 2023) as "A condition that impacts a person's thinking, feeling, or mood and may affect his/her ability to relate to others and function on a daily basis." Around one in five people experience a mental illness in a given year with 13% of all youth between eight and fifteen experiencing a severe mental disorder. These are not typical moments of stress, anxiety, or frustration but rather diagnosable conditions that get in the way of daily life. And they require interventions by experts who are well versed in a medical model of mental illness, especially in relation to young people.

The medical model of mental health is an umbrella term that focuses upon problems, symptoms, treatments and interventions aimed at the individual. Until recently, it has been a model that has paid little attention to economic, social, political, or environmental contexts in which individual students and staff struggle. The *DSM-5* (2013) diagnostic statistical manual classifies disorders and guides mental health professionals to diagnose mental disorders, identifying specific characteristics of specific disorders. Mental disorders are defined as a syndrome characterized by a clinically significant disturbance in an individual's cognitive, emotional regulation, or behavior. Mental disorders are usually associated with significant distress or disability in social, occupational, or other important activities. Administrators and educators may also want to reference the National Institutes of Mental Health (www.nimh.nih.gov) as a resource that identifies a wide range of illnesses with characteristics of each disorder.

While the medical model is essential to understand and use when diagnosing individuals and devising interventions, we encourage the use of an ecological systems model when thinking about schools, students, and staff. Every individual struggling with a mental illness or disorder lives within a particular context or system which can have massive impact on their illness as well as potential interventions. The ecological model considers the family, local community, economic situation, and larger social or political movements. It sees the individual as a part of a web of relationships and interactions with the world around them. It also takes a developmentally informed view of mental illness that takes into account age, appropriate behaviors, understanding patterns of growth and development and how they interfere with adaptive functioning and well-being. Just as crises do not occur in isolation, neither do illnesses, recovery, and healing.

Students warranting Tier 3 interventions often are experiencing a very difficult time in their functioning and in their adjustment. They may have significant mental health issues that make their everyday functioning more difficult. It may be challenging to even come to school, be around other youth, or interact with family or teachers. When considering emotional health and well-being often anxiety and depression are the two most common mental health issues affecting youth. This, coupled with other risk factors, may increase the likelihood of a mental health disorder.

Protective factors such as positive relationships with peers or adults, Tier 1 and Tier 2 supports, and strong SEL skills may help to reduce mental health issues and challenges. A holistic approach to mental health takes into account a wide range of issues, such as human development, sleeping and eating patterns, relationships, emotions, and academics. The first step is to recognize the signs of serious mental illness and then identify all of the issues so the best resources can be used to help and support the student or staff member. It is important to remember that clinical disorders are often the cause of significant physiological and psychosocial difficulties and can have a debilitating effect on psychological, social, and physical functioning, and derail learning.

A valuable resource for understanding trends locally and nationally regarding Tier 3 challenges facing adolescents and schools is the Centers for Disease Control and Prevention's (CDC, 2023a) Youth Risk Behavior Surveillance System (YRBSS). This biannual survey has collected data on over five million young people in the United States in six categories, including sexual behavior, substance use, experiences of violence, mental health, and suicidal thoughts. It provides key findings, trends, and a snapshot of adolescent health and well-being. The 2023 data also includes data on social determinants of health such as unstable housing, school connectedness, and parental monitoring. It's focused upon the goal of understanding the environment and to establish opportunities to improve upon health. The most recent report makes it clear that young people are continuing to experience high levels of distress that are leading to risky behaviors that must be addressed immediately.

COMORBIDITY

Often, we find that individuals are struggling with multiple overlapping conditions or symptoms, referred to as co-occurring conditions or comorbidity. According to *DSM-5*, comorbidity refers to how many symptoms assigned to a single disorder may occur at varying levels of severity. Concurrence of more than one disorder can result from many factors and may include physical ailments, as well as mental health conditions such as eating issues, substance abuse, anxiety and depression. It's critically important to understand the impact each condition has both separately and together upon everyday life experience, functioning, and adaptation.

There may be significant comorbidity with posttraumatic stress disorder (PTSD) and substance use disorders. Externalizing behaviors may occur as impulse control or conduct disorder. Internalized behaviors may be evident like anxiety disorders or obsessive compulsive disorder. When dealing with trauma, comorbidity is often deeply ingrained and frequently may be considered the most striking characteristic of childhood trauma and complex PTSD. It's important to recognize that symptom patterns may share common features but each individual person has a unique signature. Illnesses often do not occur in isolation but are complex and interwoven at times. Comorbidity is the realization and recognition that mental health conditions and mental illness are complex states that must be identified and understood separately and together. Intervention must be tailored to the individual student and their needs.

Let's take a look at an example of a young person struggling with co-occurring conditions. Jenny is a 16-year-old sophomore. She's highly anxious. As she entered early elementary school, she exhibited separation anxiety and worries. In middle school, she was reported to the school nurse because of concerns about eating issues and after an intervention and evaluation, Jenny was identified as having an eating disorder. She continued to struggle and in high school was seen as not only being anxious but also depressed. She tried coping with the various issues that she was struggling with, especially emotional regulation, and began using alcohol. She was frequently preoccupied with performance anxiety and her relationships with her peers.

Jenny became moody and withdrawn and when referred for an evaluation was identified as having an anxiety disorder, sometimes seen as a panic disorder and an obsessive compulsive disorder. It was also noted that she had been using alcohol and marijuana and was caught in school with substances. In an additional evaluation, she was diagnosed as having PTSD. The evaluator had discovered that Jenny had been a victim of sexual assault in a dating relationship that had been unreported. In sorting through the complexity of Jenny's situation, it became apparent that she had multiple diagnoses and co-occurring conditions.

Take a moment to think, discuss, or write about these questions:

1. Does your school have an agreed upon definition of *mental illness*?

2. When you consider students at risk, when does their behavior reach the level that warrants a more intensive intervention?

3. What are the interventions you use when students need high individual and specialized support?

4. What policies and practices do you have in place that address and support the needs of students/staff who have a mental health crisis?

ANXIETY AND DEPRESSION

Stress and anxiety are the most common challenges to a student's ability to function or completely be engaged in school life. Earlier, we explored how everyone needs to learn how to cope with normal, everyday stress and anxiety in Tier 1, and that schools should have prevention and intervention plans in place when stress and anxiety cause temporary disruptions in our lives using Tier 2 supports. In more severe cases of mental health disorders or illnesses, stress and anxiety can become the source or they can certainly impact those more difficult Tier 3 challenges.

This is why educators and parents need to have a deep understanding of how stress and anxiety impact the mind, body, and brain, as well as recognizing their signs and taking them seriously. Small preventative interventions early on can greatly reduce the chances that a person becomes more seriously affected by stress and anxiety. The most common ones we see are depression and anxiety disorder.

While we can't read minds, we can observe behavior and recognize that behavior is an important form of communication. Understanding mental illness and the wide range of disorders that may be experienced is to understand clusters of disorders as internalizing and or externalizing factors. Within the internalizing group these are disorders that are ones of anxiety, depression and somatic symptoms, while the externalizing group are often disorders of impulsivity, disruptive conflict, and substance use symptoms. The externalizing group will include disorders that relate to conduct, addiction, and impulse control, underscoring the importance of assessment and addressing comorbidity. This categorization is useful in considering the response to illnesses that can be characterized as depressed mood, anxiety, or other physiological or cognitive characteristics.

Here we're underscoring a holistic, multidimensional approach which takes into account the environment and the whole person physiologically, biologically, and psychologically.

Anxiety disorders include generalized anxiety disorder, social anxiety disorder, separation disorder, panic disorder, obsessive compulsive disorder, and specific phobias. Anxiety is the most common mental health issue according to the Anxiety Disorder Association of America. In 2020, anxiety disorders affected 25.1% of young people. The median age of onset of anxiety disorders is 11 years. According to the National Alliance of Mental Illness (NAMI), 50% of all lifetime mental illness begins by age fourteen, and in the United States one in six youth ages six through seventeen experience mental health disorders each year. However, a little over 50% of these youth receive treatment, underscoring the need for early intervention. Anxiety disorders most commonly show up in schools as school refusal, stomach aches, nervous ticks, uncontrolled outbursts, inability to communicate, substance use, self-harm, and suicidal ideation.

Sadness is a common emotion. But deep sadness that lasts more than two weeks can become diagnosed as clinical depression. Depression can refer to a wide range of mental health problems and exists along a continuum. The symptoms can vary in intensity, frequency, and duration, significantly impacting social and personal functioning. Depression and depressive symptoms include feelings of sadness, loneliness, self-harm, and suicidal ideation. The problems may not be as apparent to anyone except the individual experiencing them, with more subtle externalizing behaviors. Categories of depression in the *DSM-5* include major depression disorder, seasonal affective disorder, and mood disorders.

According to the Centers for Disease Control (2023b), 13% of teens have one depressive episode by age seventeen. Unfortunately, 60% of those adolescents received no treatment for their depression. The National Institute for Mental Health (NIMH, n.d.) reports that major depressive disorder is more prevalent in women than in men. Major depressive disorder is the leading cause of disability in the United States for ages 15 to 44. This means that we not only need to be aware of depression in adolescents, but also in staff, teachers, and parents. Depression may be seen as early as preschool and reappear in childhood and adolescence.

There are a number of mental health and physical health issues that are also connected with depression and include conduct disorders, anxiety disorders, ADHD, learning disabilities, and physical health issues. In schools, depression can be seen as deep sadness lasting more than two weeks, withdrawing from activities, loss of relationships, changes in mood or diet, weight loss, self-injury, substance abuse, or suicidal ideation.

While anxiety and depression are separate conditions, they can both be experienced at the same time. For example, people with a depressive diagnosis can also be diagnosed with an anxiety disorder. Students who have gone through traumatic events may not only be anxious but they may also be depressed and the feelings may last for significant periods of time. It's also important to recognize the complexity and the multidimensional aspects of a person's life, including culture and context, as it relates to comorbidity. As we will see in the rest of this chapter, there are many serious Tier 3 challenges we see in schools that are rooted in issues of anxiety and depression.

SCHOOL REFUSAL

School refusal is a condition that affects roughly 2% to 5% of children who refuse to come to school due to anxiety or depression. It can be relatively mild and seen in kindergarten students as separation anxiety or more severe when students miss prolonged periods of time away from school, which may be weeks or months. Recognizing that school refusal is not school truancy and being impacted by other situations or conditions like homelessness or pregnancy are key to intervention.

The presenting issue is often seen in avoidance behavior and frequently the result of anxiety—social anxiety, separation anxiety, or performance anxiety. The anxiety may be related to competition, test-taking or other real or perceived difficulties. The underlying dynamics of school refusal may be defensive, an escape from threatening situations, or attentional, to gain attention from caregivers. Comorbidity factors that are frequently associated with school refusal include anxiety disorders, such as generalized anxiety disorder, excessive and persistent worry, panic disorder, obsessive compulsive disorder, posttraumatic stress disorder, depression and or physical complaints. Most common warning signs include frequent absences or frequent visits to the nurse without apparent signs of a physical illness, and frequent requests to go home or calls home during the school day. It's also important to consider changes in patterns of sleep, eating, mood, and various domains of physical health and well-being.

In order to better assess if a student is struggling with school refusal, it is critical to understand the motive and meaning of the behavior, what need is not met, or the skill that needs to be developed. Assessment also takes into account the environment and whether the school's culture is unresponsive, unwelcoming, or unsafe (e.g., bullying). These conditions will impact the emotional experience of coming to school. Assessment should also include observations, interviews, and attendance or school records in order to understand the patterns in the student's behavior and underlying contributing factors. Family and environmental conditions can also indicate whether the refusal to come to school is impacted by contributing factors and conditions.

With the goal of improving school attendance, interventions need to be collaborative and team oriented. Students should be counseled by integrating cognitive and behavioral skills, techniques and strategies like mindfulness, relaxation techniques, self-talk, and contracts. Parent support and skill-building strategies are likely to support school attendance. When there are significant somatic or physical complaints, support from medical professionals and the student's physician may be warranted. When students miss school frequently, an early intervention plan is the optimal approach. It is important to develop a coordinated structure and routines, including a coordinated reentry plan which identifies key staff members for support, staff who are accessible and providing a safe haven, and a physical "home base" in the building. The National Institute of Mental Health, as well as the Anxiety Disorder Association of America, are two organizations that provide excellent resources and research on how to best help students who are experiencing school refusal.

PAUSE AND REFLECT

Take a moment to think, discuss, or write about these questions:

1. What are the major forces affecting young people in your school that might impact anxiety and depression?

2. Does your staff have a good understanding of anxiety and depression?

3. What is your process for managing students who have school refusal issues?

TRANSITIONS

Change and transitions occur throughout our lives and can trigger feelings of anxiety and stress. This is doubly true for individuals who are already struggling with anxiety, depression, or trauma. School leaders need to pay close attention to the many moments of transition in the lives of our children. These could be the start or end of a school year, arriving or leaving the school for the day, or the movement from classroom to classroom through hallways. Transitions occur through development and are significant periods of time that require attention. We need to pay attention to the impact of the environment and how it may support, help, or hinder adjustment and adaptation.

Students who transfer into a new school or leave the safety of their current school often report high emotions and difficulties managing that kind of change. We also have students who are making a transition from home to school or hospital to school after a prolonged illness or absence, sometimes due to tragedy, loss, or trauma. Change events can have the same impact. This could be a change in family dynamics with the arrival of a new child or the death of a beloved family member or a move to a new community. Societal changes can also impact people in this way. The last several years have seen massive political, social, and health crises that challenge all of us but can trigger additional stress and anxiety in individuals struggling with mental illness.

These kinds of transitions, transitional events, and experiences have an impact upon us. They are stressful and lead to feelings of uncertainty and loss, requiring an adjustment in how we live or cope with changes. Consider not only the transitional event in and of itself but the impact, implications, and long-standing consequences.

Think about a student who has been hospitalized; who might be returning from chronic illness, surgery, or acute illness; or a student who may be struggling with substance use, eating disorders, bipolar disorder, depression, or suicidal ideation. These are significant crisis events. Returning to school will require transitional support. Take into account the risk factors as well as protective factors surrounding the child and use that information to design appropriate interventions. It's here that a safety net of services that addresses the needs of students who are at risk is essential. We also need to consider that when significant intervention like a hospitalization has occurred, the goal is often safety and stabilization. Time is needed for recovery.

SUBSTANCE USE

Throughout this text, we've been focusing upon risk factors, elements of the world around an individual that might cause harm, and protective factors, those things that support and help individuals. When considering risk factors for substance use, it is important to look at both internal factors as well as the environment. Although it is not uncommon for youth to experiment with substances, many do not go on to develop substance abuse issues.

Some areas to consider when assessing for substance abuse is the type of substance being used, how much of it is used, and how often. It is important to consider the relationship that the person has with the substance and any past family history. The most common substances young people experiment with include nicotine, alcohol, marijuana, and prescription drugs. Over the past decade, there has been a dramatic increase in the rates of vaping in middle and high school. Many times, these substances can lead to experimentation with more serious drugs and narcotics. In 2022, 11% of eighth graders, 21.5% of tenth graders, and 32% of 12th graders reported using illicit drugs in the past year, according to the National Institutes on Drug Abuse (NIDA; 2022).

In the mental health field, experts refer to substance use on a continuum from experimentation to abuse to dependence to addiction. Substances can include alcohol or drugs. Dependence often refers to issues of frequency and need. Addiction is the most significant and intense form of substance abuse and puts youth at most risk of harm. Addiction has a significant impact upon and may cause significant damage to the person's body, brain, and mind, as well as psychological functioning. In the *DSM-5*, *substance use disorders* are defined as repetitive recurrent use of drugs or alcohol that cause significant impairment to mental health functioning and failures to meet responsibilities. Keep in mind that comorbidity or co-occurring conditions like anxiety, depression, or attention deficit disorder can be intertwined with substance use.

Throughout our Tier 1 level focus upon mental health, we have addressed the mind, body, brain connection and brain functioning. It is crucial for everyone to recognize that substance use has an impact upon brain development and can impair brain functioning as it relates to decision-making, emotional regulation, and other executive functioning skills. External and environmental risk factors related to substance use include negative peer influences, family history of substance use, and access to substances. Ironically, many of these can also be powerful forces in discouraging young people from experimenting or using drugs or alcohol. Protective factors include positive, prosocial involvement and role-modeling from family members, peers, and community members.

Open and honest communication between parents and kids can go a long way toward getting substance use out into the open and to provide young people with accurate information. We can also reduce or eliminate easy access to drugs, alcohol, and nicotine products. Studies have shown that the longer we can delay a young person trying one of these, the smaller the impact on their bodies and brains (Odgers et al., 2008).

It is also important to note here the role substance use has in connection to mental illness and other Tier 3 challenges. In some instances, when trying to cope with a mental illness, people may try to self-medicate using drugs or alcohol. In assessing what is happening to a student or staff member, it may be necessary to unpack an array of issues to determine why the individual is using or abusing a substance. Did the substance use lead to other Tier 3 issues or is the substance being used to cope with some Tier 3 challenge? We have worked directly with young people who have attempted suicide or died accidently by overdosing on drugs. It is sometimes difficult to figure out in cases like these what the core problem is so a potential intervention or solution can be attempted.

PAUSE AND REFLECT

Take a moment to think, discuss, or write about these questions:

1. How many transitions do your students make each day? Each year? What do you due to support them in these crucial moments?

2. What policies, procedures, or practices do you have at your school to prevent or intervene with substance use?

3. How do you educate and support students and staff about substance use and address the wide range of needs?

DISORDERED EATING

As we've considered risk behaviors, one question is when does it raise to the threshold of a clinical problem that requires clinical interventions. One of those risk behaviors is disordered eating. Eating disorders are characterized by a disturbance of eating or eating related behaviors. These include and may result in excessive consumption or a lack of significant consumption that significantly impairs physical health or psychosocial functioning. Diagnostic categories include anorexia nervosa, bulimia nervosa, disorders avoidant, and restrictive food intake disorders. Physical signs include restrictive eating, bingeing, purging, overexercising, weight loss or gain, preoccupation with one's physical appearance or the physical appearance of others.

According to NAMI (2023) and the National Association of Anorexia Nervosa and Associated Disorders (2023), at least thirty million people of all ages, genders and ethnicities suffer from an eating disorder in the United States. It is twice as prevalent among females than males, with a greater number of cases occurring in adolescent and older kids. Eating disorders have the highest mortality rate of any mental illness.

An essential aspect of understanding eating disorders is to identify symptoms and characteristics that cause significant distress or impairment in relationships and functioning in day-to-day life activities. Screening and assessing for eating disorders should consider contributing factors and problems, for example obsessive thoughts about food and body weight, the impact it has upon physical health, and signs of compulsive behaviors like overexercising.

As with many of the mental health issues we've been addressing, it is critical to look for co-occurring behaviors and comorbidity. As noted with assessment of psychological difficulty, there are diagnostic criteria to consider that are inclusionary and exclusionary. A clinical assessment would consider a range of diagnostic features and would take into account family, environment, physical, behavioral, social, and psychological factors.

FOCUS ON SELF-HARM

Another mental disorder that mostly impacts adolescents is self-harm or "nonsuicidal self-injury," which is intentional injury to one's body without suicidal intent. It is considered an attempt to relieve intolerable emotional pain believing that the behavior will alleviate the pain. Self-harm can be a way of communicating a sense of anguish, as relief from emotional pain, interpersonal difficulties, or to induce a more positive state. It often starts in early teens and can continue for an extended period of time.

Self-harm can include indirect forms, like the excessive use of substances both legal and illegal, and more direct forms, like ingesting nondigestible objects, cutting, hitting, pinching, bruising, punching objects, or hair-pulling. It can be caused by depression, low self-esteem, abuse, or anxiety. We know that approximately two million cases are reported annually in the United States, affecting 15% of youths and 17% to 35% of young adults. One in five are female; one in seven are male. Half of those injuring themselves have some kind of trauma history (Hauber et al., 2019; Klonsky et al., 2014). As with many of the mental health conditions we've addressed, we want to understand the behavior, its meaning, function, and emotional state.

An effective school-based intervention is dialectical behavioral therapy (DBT) for adolescents. It provides a guide for working with children or adolescents struggling with control of behaviors and emotions. It teaches five sets of skills that correspond to five major problem areas with emotional dysregulation, including mindfulness, distress tolerance, emotional regulation, and interpersonal effectiveness. Small groups supported by a social worker can also be very effective as an intervention. Early identification of self-harming behaviors is critical as these can indicate or lead to more serious issues such as suicidal ideation and suicide. Staff training on signs of self-injury is a key early warning system, as is a school culture where peers feel comfortable telling a trusted adult.

SUICIDAL IDEATION

Ben, a high school junior, felt as though he was a burden to others and was increasingly feeling overwhelmed and helpless. He had begun to believe he had little reason to live and started to think about harming himself. Ben's behavior included his increased use of alcohol and marijuana. He began exploring and researching ways of killing himself. He withdrew from friends and was isolating himself. Ben tended to vacillate between sleeping too much and not getting enough sleep. He had increased signs of depression and began making overtures and attempts to say goodbye to family and friends.

Ben is an example of one of the thousands of young people across the United States who are thinking about suicide or making a plan to kill themselves. In 2023, the Centers for Disease Control reported that almost 50,000 people committed suicide in the past year, the highest number ever recorded (Stobbe, 2023). A nationwide survey of students in Grades 9 through 12 in 2017 found that 17.7% of students reported seriously considering suicide, 14.6% reported making a plan, and 8.6% reported trying to take their lives in the year preceding the survey (CDC report on Trends in the Prevalence of Suicide). Suicide is among the leading causes of death for adolescents and young adults (National Institutes of Mental Health [NIMH], 2023).

Here are some important definitions and distinctions related to suicide and suicidal ideation:

- Suicidal ideation: thoughts of suicide and/or wanting to take one's own life
- Suicidal behavior: actions by one who is considering or planning their own death
- Suicide attempt: Any action taken with the intent of ending one's life whether it results in injury or not
- Suicide: intentionally causing one's own death

Making a distinction between these components of ideation, intent, and action helps assess behavior, likelihood, and severity, and how to start building an intervention plan (Singer & O'Brien, 2015).

Suicidal ideation is having thoughts or preoccupation with suicide or death. This preoccupation may be the result of a suicide in the person's life, a family history of suicide, depression, or mental illness. There may be stressful events or loss in the person's life. Alcohol and drug use is often connected with suicide and suicidal ideation. Recognizing the warning signs of risky behavior levels of risk, and of mental illness is critical. One of the most significant factors you may want to consider is what access the person has to lethal means. In 2020, firearms accounted for half of the suicide deaths in the United States (NIMH, 2023).

Many but not all individuals will talk about death or suicide to friends, family members, or anyone with a close relationship. It is essential that we change culture so people are willing to not only talk about their thoughts but others feel comfortable telling an adult that they are worried about their friend. Referrals of peers to a social worker, teacher, nurse, or administrators can literally be the difference between life and death.

It is critical to recognize that students can be in many different types of crises but not all are suicidal. Schools should have a framework in place that recognizes that not all crises are alike. It means having processes, policies, and procedures in place to respond, distinguish, and determine how you can help students to manage extraordinarily or really intense experiences. Recognizing the signs of crisis and what puts a student in an emotional crisis when they may or may not be suicidal requires schools to think in a sophisticated way about these issues and respond in a precise way. This will avoid overreacting but also respond proactively when a student or adult are contemplating suicide or self-injury. Large-scale surveys like the Youth Risk Behavior Survey (2023) from the CDC or school climate surveys can give administrators a "big picture" of suicidal ideation and other risk behaviors. Screeners that identify individuals can also be used by trained clinical social workers and psychologists to get a clearer sense of whether a student is suicidal and how to best intervene.

If you or anyone you know needs support and someone to talk with, call any of these support phone numbers:

National Suicide Helpline number: 988

National Suicide Prevention Hotline: 1-800-273-8255 or Text 1-847-716-2252

SAMSHA Helpline: 1-800-662-HELP

NAMI Helpline: 1-833-626-4244

PAUSE AND REFLECT

Take a moment to think, discuss, or write about these questions:

1. When considering risk behavior, where do you think students reach the level that warrants more intensive interventions?

2. What is your screening and referral process for students who are really struggling?

3. What do you think is the level of understanding about self-harm and suicide among your staff?

4. What types of student awareness and staff development programs do you have in place to address suicide prevention?

SUICIDE

Kat, a sixteen-year-old girl, missed the majority of her freshman and sophomore years and quit the track team due to chronic migraines. After going to several doctors and trying many medications, she still experienced severe migraines. Kat was falling very behind in school and was withdrawn from her close group of friends. She was very popular but it was common for her not to leave her house for days at a time, with no interaction with peers. Her friends would still stop by and call every week but she increasingly became more distant and isolated. She stated to her parents that life wasn't worth living and that she felt that she would never get back to normal. Her father found her in the bathroom unconscious. Next to her was an empty bottle of her medication. She had ended her life.

We've already discussed some of the alarming statistics about suicidal attempts and deaths in the United States. In many ways, suicide death flies under the radar compared to other deaths. The media is more apt to report on deaths by violence than suicides and there continues to be a stigma regarding talking about suicide. In 2020, the number of deaths by suicide were twice that of homicides (NIMH, 2023). We know that females account for most of nonfatal attempts, usually through medications or poison, and that almost 80% of people who die are male. Almost all who attempt suicide suffer from some form of mental illness, most often depression. Impulsivity or alcohol and drug use are found in 25% of suicides (National Alliance on Mental Illness, 2023). There is no single pathway to suicide. There are many factors that can increase risk, including race, gender, class, and other mental illnesses. The strongest risk factor is a prior attempt. Another important risk factor is whether there is a gun in the home, as well as easy access to other means of death.

Educators must recognize that bouts of anxiety, sadness, and despair are normal reactions to loss, rejection, or disappointment but suicide is an intentional act that is centered on causing one's own death. Adolescents are a particularly vulnerable population as it is developmentally a time of change and transition. They are also pushing the boundaries and taking risks in ways that may make them more open to suicidal ideation or behavior. We have also explored the concept of comorbidity and how other behaviors and mental illnesses, such as depression, stress, anxiety, self-harm, and substance abuse, can complicate a young person's perspective and ability to cope. It's important to recognize that 85% of students report never having had serious thoughts about suicide (NIMH, 2023).

SUICIDE INTERVENTION

Assessing a suicide situation and using that assessment to determine a course of action is one of the most important steps in an intervention plan. The primary goal of the suicide risk assessment is to determine the level of risk. The screening may consider a range from no risk to extreme risk with the focus being the goal of short-term stabilization, potential obstacles to safety, and what helpful intervention strategies are needed. Assessment for ideation through a critical suicide risk takes into account intention, planning, previous attempts, and other factors. An assessment of all risk behavior interventions must be tailored to the individual student's needs. As noted, risk is categorized according to specific family, environmental, social, emotional, and ethnographic factors that take into account age, gender, ethnicity, sexual orientation, and access to means, as well as life stressors. An assessment also takes into account protective factors looking at strengths and resources in the school, at home, and in the community such as peer support, school programming, and access to local medical resources (Erbacher et al., 2015; Singer & O'Brien, 2015).

One of the most important protective factors to prevent a suicide is having a strong support system, which would include early identification and intervention, including home, school, and peer groups. Support systems that specifically target kids who are exhibiting suicidal ideation can be very successful in preventing death or injury. Educators need to recognized the signs of suicide and mental health professionals need to carefully diagnose what is happening so a solid treatment plan can be implemented quickly. Any school that wants to take suicide prevention seriously will create a culture where suicidal ideation is discussed openly and safely. They will also implement strong assessments of student behavior and processes to respond, and provide resources and support.

Let's take a look at how this might play out in a school's comprehensive Mental Health Action Plan as we've discussed throughout this book.

In a Multi-Tiered Systems of Support (MTSS) model, underlying interventions focus upon building a community that is inclusive, and having policies, practices and procedures that are well defined, clearly communicated, and embedded in practice. Tier 1 interventions include awareness and prevention curriculums that are taught in health classes but also are reinforced through social emotional learning skills and strategies throughout the school. For example, in 2017, the Illinois State Board of Education and state legislature passed what is known as "Anne Marie's Law," which requires that all school boards in the state enact a policy that teaches suicide awareness and prevention education to all students and staff with the goal of early identification and referral of students possibly at risk of suicide. This can happen in classes and advisories for students, as well as in professional learning workshops for staff. Prevention strategies include not only suicide awareness, help seeking behaviors, and supportive resources but also focus on well-being. Primary prevention activities are skill based in which students are taught about depression and suicide prevention but also where and how to access resources and support. They are taught about coping skills, building self-esteem, self-efficacy, communication skills, and problem-solving. All students should be taught about the brain and stress management as well as healthy behaviors, all in relation to suicidal ideation and suicide.

Tier 2 strategies for suicide prevention would include using a universal screener, a program like Signs of Suicide, as well as more individualized screeners used by social workers and psychologists. Specific staff development and learning would delve into the neuroscience, human development, and research about suicidal ideation, suicide, and the comorbidity with other mental illnesses. Specialized student support teams made up of teachers, social workers, psychologists, nurses, and administrators would dive into individual student issues and design skill-based interventions with follow up to make sure each student is supported and monitored. Schools need to also take a close look at the curriculum and instruction in the classroom, as well as their communication and marketing. What messages are being sent and read about suicide? How are we educating local and national media about suicide? Teachers and school leaders should also partner with parent organizations, local social service organizations, clergy, and hospitals to coordinate suicide prevention and response efforts.

Tier 3 strategies should focus on crisis intervention and coordination when a suicide attempt or successful suicide has occurred. This includes having policies, procedures, and practices that are in response to risk behaviors and suicidal attempts but also take into account procedures for following a death of a student or adult. This involves not just having a crisis plan in place but recognizing the impact of such an event, both in the school and in the community, responding to the rippling effect of a suicidal death, both short and long term. It means having a crisis intervention plan but also a postvention plan following a death. Thought should be given to what official messages the school puts out, the role the school will play in any immediate events, and the long-term requests for memorials and remembrances. Some of these same processes can be used whenever there is a death or tragedy in the school or community. However, a suicide death brings with it some unique difference that need to be thought through ahead of time.

PAUSE AND REFLECT

Take a moment to think, discuss, or write about these questions:

1. How open are students, staff, and the community to discussions of suicidal ideation and suicide? What have been your experiences with suicide?

2. What is your school's process for assessing and responding to suicidal ideation or a suicide? What existing systems could help? What systems need to be created?

3. What programs do you have in place that raise student and staff awareness about suicide, and how to access support and resources?

FOCUS ON DISRUPTIVE BEHAVIOR DISORDERS

A child's behavior expresses meaning and it is often a form of communication. The question is what does the behavior mean and express. Disruptive behavior disorders represent ongoing patterns related to a group of behavioral issues. These patterns are often seen in classrooms as uncooperative and hostile behaviors toward others and have a significant impact upon the student's daily functioning. They may include ignoring rules, disruption or defiance, dysregulation, and difficulty managing emotions. Observable characteristics may be anger expressed through aggressive behavior, irritable mood, violent and aggressive acts that might cause harm, destruction, threats, and violation of rules. As with many of the mental health challenges that have been addressed thus far, disruptive behavior disorders frequently are co-occurring with other disorders such as substance use, self-injury, stress, and trauma.

In the *Diagnostic and Statistical Manual of Mental Disorders,* 5th ed (*DSM-5*; American Psychiatric Association, 2013). these types of behavioral concerns are referred to as disruptive impulse control and conduct disorders. Basically they're describing problems with self-control of behavior and emotions. They involve problems of emotional regulation that are evidenced through behaviors that violate the rights of others, bring students into significant conflict with authority figures, and focus on self-control. They may include oppositional defiant disorder, impulse control problems, and conduct disorder. The central features of these disorders are externalized behavior and frequent and persistent patterns that relate to anger and irritability. Oppositional defiant disorder is a recurrent pattern of impulsivity and anger for six months or longer that significantly impacts relationships and health. Conduct disorder is indicative of delinquency and aggression toward others. This may include incidents of bullying, harassment, and delinquency.

When considering disruptive behaviors, we're not looking at isolated incidents of misbehavior or minor behavioral infractions within schools. We're looking at patterns of behaviors that have been evidenced over a period of six months with marked distress and impairment, keeping in mind that mental illness is complex and exists along a spectrum. We need to consider the impact upon functioning and severity and the range from minimal to extreme. For a conduct disorder, we consider persistent violation of others' rights or local social rules including property destruction, lying, theft, or illegal activities. For an intermittent explosive disorder, we're looking at recurrent verbal or physical outbursts or out of character and disproportionate responses to whatever stressors they are facing.

We need to stay aware of how psychological, emotional, and social functioning are intertwined with students' problems and how issues that we see in and through their behavior are expressions of needs or underdeveloped skills. It is also important to assess and consider how the individual and others and the environment can influence psychological, emotional, and academic functioning. Many of our students who have behavioral and psychological issues in schools often have a mental health history and a trauma history. Considering the key trauma-informed questions raised in this text provides an opportunity to develop trauma-informed practices and restorative interventions.

CHILDHOOD TRAUMA

We've already explored the physical and psychological impact of immediate trauma on the mind, brain, and body. Trauma also impacts development, as well as how people think, feel, and relate. In the experience of trauma, it is common to have comorbid disorders and problems related to depression, substance abuse, and nonsuicidal self-injury. Trauma exists along a spectrum from minor to severe, from short term to long term. The impact of a trauma experience also changes depending on the individual, such as their age, gender, culture, coping and resiliency skills. Context, the environment, and situation also have a huge impact on how someone experiences trauma. It is important to not ask "What is wrong with you?" but rather "What is happening to you?"

Childhood experiences, both positive and negative, have a tremendous impact on future violence, victimization, health, and opportunity. As such, early experiences are an important backstory to consider when working with anyone who is struggling with mental health. Much of the foundational research in this area has been referred to as adverse childhood experiences or ACEs.

The CDC-Kaiser Permanente Adverse Childhood Experiences (ACE) Study (2023) is one of the largest investigations of childhood abuse, neglect, and later-life health and well-being. The original ACE Study was conducted at the Kaiser Institute from 1995 to 1997 with two waves of data collection. Over 17,000 health maintenance organization members from Southern California receiving physical exams completed confidential surveys regarding their childhood experiences and current health status and behaviors. The study's participants were mostly white, middle- and upper-middle class college-educated Californians with good jobs and great health care. Today, the Centers for Disease Control continues ongoing surveillance of ACEs by assessing the medical status of the study participants via periodic updates of morbidity and mortality data.

The questionnaire asked participants to identify if they had experienced any of the ten adverse childhood experiences, ranging from abuse to neglect to household dysfunction.

- Physical abuse

- Sexual abuse

- Emotional abuse

- Physical neglect

- Emotional neglect

- Living with a family member who is depressed or diagnosed with mental illness or had attempted suicide

- Living with a family member who is addicted to alcohol or another substance

- Criminal behavior in the household/a family member who is incarcerated

- Mother treated violently/intimate partner violence

- Divorce or parental separation

Dr. Nadine Burke-Harris, former surgeon general for the state of California, calls the ACE's study the most important study of the 20th century and needs to be a bigger part of the conversation about how childhood trauma impacts the mind and body of children and adults: "The body of research sparked by the ACE Study makes it clear that adverse childhood experiences in and of themselves are a risk factor for many of the most common and serious diseases in the United States (and worldwide), regardless of income or race or access to care" (Burke-Harris, 2018).

According to the Centers for Disease Control (2023b), while 36% of the respondents reported zero ACE's, the vast majority, 63%, reported at least one ACE. Twenty-six percent of the seventeen thousand people in the ACE Study had an ACE score of one while 17% reported four or more ACEs. Researchers have found that as a person's ACE score increases, so does the risk of disease, social, and emotional problems. Lower ACE scores(1–3) can lead to academic, social, emotional, and physical impairment in young people and adults. With an ACE score of four or more, things start getting more alarming. The likelihood of chronic pulmonary lung disease increases 390%; hepatitis 240%; depression 460%; and the chance of suicide increases by over 1000%. Over the past 25 years the ACE's study has been replicated and expanded additional criteria, including community violence, homelessness, discrimination, foster care, bullying, repeated life-threatening or health related illnesses, death of caregivers, loss of a caregiver, verbal or physical violence, and incarceration (Karatekin & Hill, 2018).

Trauma can involve a wide range of events that we've discussed earlier, such as natural disasters, human-caused events, community or family acts of violence, accidents, medical emergencies, sudden deaths, and prolonged illnesses. We discussed toxic stress, chronic stress, and cumulative stress as significant events and types of adversity to consider as we take into account mental health issues that are clearly apparent in schools. Another way we can see long-term effects of trauma is through posttraumatic stress disorders or PTSD. Keep in mind that not everyone exposed to trauma develops PTSD. For those that do, the onset of symptoms may occur soon after an event or may be triggered months or years later. PTSD is a *DSM-5* diagnosis and includes symptoms like flashbacks, a state of hyperarousal and reactivity, impaired cognitive functioning, or a sense of disassociation. The individual may shut down as a way of coping. With children, the signs of PTSD may be some type of developmental regression, withdrawal and isolation, or becoming overly clingy. They may demonstrate acting out or aggressive behavior.

Educators and school leaders must start by acknowledging trauma and its prevalence in our society. We also must recognize that the children in our schools may be dealing with long-term effects of previous childhood trauma, or they may be experiencing it right now as immediate trauma. In either situation, students are walking into schools and classrooms deeply impacted by early childhood trauma and in a dysfunctional state. It affects how they are perceiving school and peers and teachers. The prefrontal cortex may not be engaged, creating a roadblock to thinking, learning, memory, and decision-making, and when triggered, they freeze.

Trauma-informed classrooms and schools, led by trauma-informed teachers and administrators, can go a long way in creating Tier 1 and Tier 2 support systems that will help students cope with the trauma or trauma-effects they are experiencing (Craig, 2016; Jennings, 2018; Romero et al., 2018). But for some of our most impacted students, they will need higher levels of support by trained staff.

Some of the strategies we've discussed in Tier 1 and Tier 2, such as social and emotional learning curricula, circles, and student-centered classrooms are necessary to be trauma informed. Later in this chapter, we'll look more closely at an array of Tier 3 strategies that will also help support students experiencing the effects of trauma.

PAUSE AND REFLECT

Take a moment to think, discuss, or write about these questions:

1. What patterns of disruptive behavior do you experience in your school? What is your standard approach to managing disruptive behavior? Is it trauma informed? Does it take into account potential coexisting mental health issues?

2. How knowledgeable is your staff about the long-term impact of childhood trauma? Are they familiar with the ACE study?

3. In what ways could your school be changed to become trauma sensitive and aware of children experiencing current or previous trauma?

EQUITY AND MENTAL ILLNESS

Woven into each aspect of any comprehensive Mental Health Action Plan must be a deep regard for the diversity of our students and staff, and a focus on equity. SAMSHA, the Substance Abuse and Mental Health Services Administration branch of the U.S. Department of Health and Human Services, offers this definition of *equity* in regard to mental health: "Behavioral health equity is the right to access high-quality and affordable healthcare services and supports for all populations, including Black, Latino, and Indigenous and Native American persons; Asian Americans and Pacific Islanders and other persons of color; members of religious minorities; veterans and military service members; older adults; LGBTQI+ persons; persons with disabilities; persons who live in rural areas; and persons otherwise adversely affected by persistent poverty or inequality" (Substance Abuse and Mental Health Services Administration [SAMHSA], 2023).

Major discrepancies exist in our society related to accessing mental health care based on these different identities. Intersectionality provides us with an opportunity to look at individuals who carry multiple identities and highlights the complicated nature of positionality, context, power and privilege. Equity challenges us to deeply consider inclusion, diversity, and belonging. We also need to understand the context of the environment as an issue of connection, belonging, and access to mental health care.

In schools, we need to think carefully about how equity is defined and the language that we use. But more important is how we enact equity and how we feel valued and accepted. We all have similarities in how we learn but we all have unique and distinct differences. It drives our attention to fully appreciate a whole child perspective and a whole school/community approach.

In *Unearthing Joy* (2023), Gholdy Muhammad talks about many different approaches and programs in schools that address diversity, equity, inclusion, and belonging. She writes, "Equity is teaching and learning that is centered on justice, liberation, truth, and freedom, and is free of bias and favoritism. . . . A school that is truly equitable, embraces, fairness, and inclusion, and in response to students' individual needs, provides structures, systems, and practices that enable all students to reach their highest potential for personal and academic success. Equity as access, only, without addressing structural oppression/racism is an equity in its fullest" (p. 33). Certainly, a school's approach to equity is paramount in Tiers 1 and 2 but we should spend time designing our Tier 3 supports and interventions so they enact our beliefs about diversity, equity, and inclusion (Venet, 2023).

FOCUS ON NEURODIVERSITY

One issue of diversity we need to highlight, especially in schools, is neurodiversity and individual learning differences. Neurodiversity acknowledges that everyone is unique, and we all learn differently. People who learn and process information differently than others are considered to be neurodivergent learners. Recognizing that distinction is fundamental and how we consider differences and treat these students is critical. Neurodivergence focuses on understanding the variation in how the brain develops and is used. It challenges the way we understand how students experience the world. These are not problems that need to be solved or fixed. Neurodiversity challenges traditional approaches to learning and problem-solving.

Schools tend to follow a medical model and see neurodiversity as a deficit. Certainly, we must be aware of the obstacles learning disorders can cause in a traditional school context. In the *DSM-5*, there are categories of learning disorders that include reading disorders, math disorders, disorders of written expression, and nonverbal learning disabilities. Evans et al. (2015), posits that 3% to 10% of children have a diagnosis of ADHD and around 15% of people are neurodivergent, so this population of students and staff exists in our schools. But viewing them as a deficit reduces the opportunity for neurodiverse individuals from being part of our school culture and decision-making.

Veteran educator and Head of School Dr. Miriam Pike has dedicated her life to a strengths-based approach to neurodiversity, helping to found Wolcott College Prep High School in Chicago, Illinois. When designing the school, she and the staff made a conscious decision to see neurodiversity in a positive way. "We took a strength based approach. We decided to use the term learning differences, which is not without controversy, but It was an important term for us. That's saying we see differences but we're not focusing on the disability. Disability has connotations of ableism and is seen as a deficit. So we were very careful about our language and designed the curriculum to be high level with high expectations." This kind of approach is a great example of how equitable and inclusionary thinking can change the lives of all students and adults.

PAUSE AND REFLECT

Take a moment to think, discuss, or write about these questions:

1. In what ways do issues of diversity intersect with mental health in your school and community?

2. What interventions have you implemented that are specifically designed for certain groups or identities?

TIER 3 PREVENTION AND INTERVENTION

In a comprehensive Mental Health Action Plan, school leaders designing Tier 3 prevention, intervention, and response strategies should keep in mind all of the various mental health challenges and disorders we've covered in this chapter, but also the existing Tier 1 and Tier 2 strategies. While the challenges are difficult and quite complex, the larger focus on universal strategies for all students should greatly reduce the number of Tier 3 issues you are facing.

These Tier 1 and Tier 2 strategies also continue to offer important support to students who are struggling with Tier 3 issues. They should also have created a common language and common understanding of certain mental models regarding school culture, relationships, and mental health that will help. A holistic, whole-child, whole-school systems perspective on mental health has significant implications for the school community as a way of looking at stress, stressors, trauma, motivation, and behavior.

Tier 3 concerns are the most serious we experience in schools. In a continuum of care model, Tier 3 interventions address the most vulnerable, high risk students. Teachers who are trained to recognize the signs of these issues are a critical early warning system but they must then refer students to qualified nurses, counselors, psychologists, and social workers. Schools must also collaborate closely with local police, hospitals, health agencies, and non-profits who are trained in these areas. However, there are certainly Tier 3

Interventions that schools can implement that have a positive impact, especially interventions that are integrated, collaborative, and coordinated.

Mental health needs to be understood in terms of depth, complexity, and how it is embedded in all aspects of a school and life. Consider how mental health intersects with everyday life. People move back and forth, in and out of mental health, shifting between health and illness, requiring constant awareness and attention.

School Staff Expertise and Training

At the heart of everything we do in schools is a caring, well-trained staff. Administrators, teachers, and support staff provide immediate support to students struggling with severe mental health disorders and illnesses. Every educator and staff member needs to learn about mental illness and various disorders through focused professional development. They must recognize the signs of these challenges and practice how to intervene or refer a student to a specially trained staff member.

Recently, we have heard many teachers say, "But I'm not a social worker." That's true. But as a classroom teacher, it is essential to know the signs of distress, to create conditions in the classroom where all students feel safe and engaged, and to know the procedures for getting immediate help to a student who is struggling. This can occur in on-going professional development, staff meetings, and institute days.

Staff members who are trained as counselors, social workers, psychologists, nurses, and some aides must also be given ample opportunities to learn, grow, and upgrade their skills. They must keep up with the most recent changes in health care, science, and research. These educators should also be part of every discussion and decision related to the creation of systems, processes, or protocols for preventing and intervening with students struggling with Tier 3 issues.

School leaders should engage these educators in leading professional development of the staff and establishing trusting relationships with their colleagues ahead of crisis moments. School boards and administrators must staff every school building where students are present with a full-time nurse and full-time social worker. And in large schools there should be a team of these professionals, enough to provide the total student population with reasonable support on any given day.

In considering the many challenges that may be presented in supporting students with Tier 3 challenges, we also need to recognize the impact of stress on staff. Here we may need to focus upon building capacity around self-care and the recognition of secondary traumatic stress, supporting teachers who may be dealing with burnout, compassion fatigue, or their own mental health challenges. Building teacher resilience means supporting teachers in developing good coping skills and practices.

But more importantly, schools need to create the conditions that support teachers. School schedules should include time away from students for rest, reset, and sustenance. Increasing teacher preparation time, time for communicating with parents, and in-school professional learning opportunities all should be part of a mentally healthy school that supports staff, teachers, and administrators who are giving themselves to supporting struggling students.

Small Groups

As we saw in Tier 2, bringing students together in a small group to process a specific issue with a trained adult can be a very powerful intervention. This is also true of more serious mental health challenges like we have explored in Tier 3 with two notable exceptions. First, given the serious nature of some of these topics, the staff leading these groups should have additional training or be specifically social workers, school psychologists, or professionals from outside the school agencies.

Second, the group process being used and goals are even more focused on skill-building. An example would be to take any particular problem —communication problems, anger management, stress management—and identify the skills that would help the student function more effectively and appropriately in school. Then, teach the skill by breaking down the skills into steps, practicing it multiple times. Remain intentional and explicit using strategies of modeling, homework, and role playing, putting it in a situational context.

Groups are dynamic and are impactful interventions at Tiers 1 and 2. They should be focused upon goals and tasks. For example, a social skills group would focus upon communication, awareness, assertiveness, cooperation or responsibility. A group on relationships would focus on communication, listening, assertiveness, and conflict mediation skills.

An example of a Tier 3 small group is one that focuses upon emotional regulation and skill-building. The use of dialectical behavioral therapy (DBT) has been utilized in a variety of settings and is adaptable for use in schools (Rathus et al., 2014, 2020). It can be applied as a primary, secondary or tertiary prevention framework. Students who are highly vulnerable to risk behaviors, may have difficulty controlling behavior, managing emotions, impulse control, self-harm behavior, substance use disorder, impulsivity, or interpersonal problems are candidates for a DBT group. The skills include teaching mindfulness, distress tolerance, and emotional regulation. The curriculum is module based, psychoeducational, collaborative, and can be adapted and tailored to the distinct needs of the group. It can also be useful to engage parents as well as school teams.

Bridges Transition Program

Bethany is a sophomore girl who has struggled for over a year with anxiety, cutting, and bulimia. Several teachers, her counselor, and the assistant principal have all worked individually and collectively to support Bethany as her grades slipped and her attendance waned. Her parents have been overwhelmed and unsure what to do. Two weeks ago, Bethany had a breakdown and was hospitalized after taking an overdose of prescription drugs.

After several days in the hospital, Bethany was sent home. The school counselor reaches out to her parents and lets them know that the school has a plan to transition Bethany back to school once she feels she is ready. The counselor will meet with all of her teachers to make sure they are ready for her return and won't pile on a lot of homework and tests. She will also have the chance, at any time, to sit in the counselor's office if she needs a break or just a quiet moment from the noise in the halls. The counselor asks Bethany and her parents to set up a day and time for a reentry meeting so everyone is clear on the transition plan. They will also meet again after a few days to check in and see how Bethany is doing. Teachers will be asked once a week to submit a short summary about her progress in class.

Often, after a student is absent or hospitalized for a prolonged period, we assume that they are ready to resume normal school activities. However, the transition back to school is highly individualized so some students may need more support than others. A Bridges program, like the one described above, creates a support system for students by coordinating communication and an intervention plan between the student, their family, and their teachers during those critical first days or weeks back. Sometimes, this means some staff time dedicated to serving in this coordination role but it can also include a room or space in the school where students can have a "home base" during their transition back to school.

By easing the student back to school, you can increase the possibility that they will continue their progress back to a regular school day. Some schools have found this attention to transition through a bridges-style protocol can also help with students struggling with physical ailments, such as broken legs or mono, as well as family tragedies, trauma, or life events.

Take a moment to think, discuss, or write about these questions:

1. What professional development do you provide to staff about mental illness and Tier 3 issues?

2. How are you engaging students in supporting each other in regard to mental and physical health?

3. How are you helping individual students as they transition in and out of school due to hospitalizations and absences?

Parent and Family Support

Schools can provide enormous support to parents and families who have children struggling with serious mental health challenges. We have already looked at how a Mental Health Action Plan at your school can provide parents with important baseline information about mental health and related issues in Tiers 1 and 2. Doing this not only prepares parents and family members to be positive forces in the lives of their children but it also can help reduce the stigma that surrounds mental illness, and to create a culture of caring in the school and community.

It is also crucial to help parents notice the early signs of mental illness and to be prepared to support a child who faces sometimes life-threatening struggles. Parent workshops or "Parent University" short courses, book studies, newsletters, and websites can provide parents and families with written information and valuable learning opportunities. These can also be relatively inexpensive endeavors and can be repeated every year or two.

More intense support can come in the form of a small group for parents, again focused on a specific Tier 3 topic and with the purpose of both processing the topic but also teaching skills that can be used in the home to support a struggling child. Examples of parent small groups could focus on such topics as a child struggling with addiction or an eating disorder, adolescent depression, self-injury, or suicidal ideation. Individual counseling may be important in some situations, with school staff working one-on-one with the parent or guardian to think through scenarios or to practice skills.

Some schools have created a parent hotline or email mailbox that is closely monitored for immediate response or support. By providing support and education to our parents and families, we can ensure that our efforts across the school and at home are aligned for maximum effectiveness.

Community Organizations and Resources

"It takes a village to raise a child." This African proverb is a powerful reminder for educators managing the mental health challenges facing students. Too often, we see schools as islands unto themselves when they are surrounded by local, state, and national organizations and institutions that can help. Some of our schools are sitting in "resource rich" communities and don't build relationships with those organizations. Other schools find themselves in sparse resource environments and would love to have more.

In doing a landscape analysis of your school and local context, it is crucial to first identify any local group, organization, company, or institution that might be helpful or interested in helping your school. The next step is to reach out and build relationships with them. Share who you are and what challenges you are facing to see how they might be able to help. Donations of food to a teacher professional development workshop or institute day, interns and students teacher from local or regional universities, cowriting a federal grant with the county hospital to fund workshops, and hosting events at a local YMCA or senior center are all examples of schools and community resources coming together.

As a principal, imagine being faced with a tragedy such as a student suicide death or a car accident and being able to call one person and suddenly have an entire team of mental health first responders arrive at the school. This kind of resource is called a Community Response Network and it should be a part of every comprehensive mental health action plan. A Community Response Network brings together local educators, administrators, social workers, therapists, psychologists, clergy, civic leaders, health-care providers, and first responders. They should meet regularly and get to know each other and their organizations well. These meetings should give everyone a chance to share the strengths and challenges of their organization, and to identify how they might help in an emergency.

An initial task should be to create a constantly updated communication protocol with phone and text numbers. This provides the avenue for mobilizing the network quickly and precisely. It can also be used to share accurate information professionally, aiding in dispelling rumors while also maintaining discretion and sensitivity. In a crisis situation, members of the network can coordinate across agencies to make sure no one is duplicating efforts or causing additional confusion. For this reason, members of the network should be part of all crisis intervention planning, training, and assessment.

One of the best examples of a community organization working on behalf of children, schools and families is Erika's Lighthouse. Erika's Lighthouse was founded in 2004 after a student suicide death to shine a light on one of the most important Tier 3 issues: teen depression. They do this through an amazing array of activities and resources. For students, they have a number of great articles and videos to educate teens about depression. They also offer a way for students to form clubs in their schools to help educate each other. For parents, Erika's Lighthouse (2023) has produced one of the best parent handbooks on childhood and teen depression we've ever seen. It is available for free on the Erika's Lighthouse website as a downloadable PDF. For schools, Erika's Lighthouse offers "The Lighthouse Curriculum," a video-based high school classroom curriculum that can help educators open up conversations about mental health, depression, and suicide. They can also come to your school to do in-service workshops with staff and teachers about these topics.

The staff at Erika's Lighthouse offers these suggestions for implementing a Mental Health Action Plan at your school that encompasses Top 3 Aspects of School Mental Health.

- Tier 1: Universal programming is the foundation of any effective mental health identification and intervention plan. A shared common vocabulary between students, educators and families is essential for Tier 2 and Tier 3 interventions to work. Tier 1 programs not only improve Tier 2 and Tier 3 outcomes, but reduce the incidence and severity of students that are being identified experiencing mental distress.

- Tier 1 programming should be expansive and coordinated with messaging that is integrated between stakeholders in a way that normalizes conversations. Educators should be prepared to respond and connect students, families ready to support their children and students can empathize and understand their peers.

- The answer to improving mental health issues among youth and reducing Tier 2 challenges, such as substance use, absenteeism, and a host of others, is student and school connectedness. Students must be seen, heard, feel valued, cared for, and connected. The ability for students to be able to identify a trusted adult and have the knowledge and vocabulary to speak to that adult is key.

In terms of how all of these coordinated activities between schools and outside organizations can help with the most severe Tier 3 challenges, Peggy Kubert, the former clinical director of Erika's Lighthouse, recalled their work with the school Erika attended when she committed suicide: "Five years after Erika died, I interviewed the Mental Health Team at [her school] and asked what had changed over these past years. Overwhelmingly, everyone said collaboration. Everyone from the front desk greeter, to the educators, to the mental health staff—everyone used the same vocabulary and kept on eye out for symptoms of emotional distress that any student might be experiencing. And they knew who to share that information with. This collaboration felt like a safety net was formed around students."

Take a moment to think, discuss, or write about these questions:

1. What resources do you provide to parents and families about child development, learning, neuroscience, mental and physical health?

2. What community and state organizations do you currently work with?

3. What other resources in your area could you connect with to provide support to students and staff?

Crisis Response

Events in schools over the past 20 years have moved us all into annual crisis response planning and practice. Students and staff are faced with a parade of emergency response drills related to fires, inclement weather, natural disasters, and intruders on campus. It is absolutely necessary to not only practice these emergency procedures regularly but it is also important to have a solid crisis response plan and procedures.

The first step is to actually have a plan! This should be a written document that is available electronically and in print, and made available to every member of the staff. It should detail what standard procedures are in an emergency and list specific names, titles, and contact information for individuals responsible for each step. It should also be written in line with local, state, and federal guidelines for emergency response.

We strongly suggest working closely with the local police, fire, and medical staff, as well as regional and state authorities, when writing your crisis response plan. A template for such a plan should be available from your state board of education or local fire and police officials. It is also imperative that you practice the plan with those local authorities, both in table-top, role-playing scenarios and through in-person training exercises when students are not in attendance. Both of these kinds of exercises allow both school personnel and outside authorities to practice and troubleshoot any problems with the crisis response plan.

From a mental health perspective, it is also important to infuse mental health support into your crisis response plan. For example, how are you involving social workers and psychologists into the writing and planning of your crisis plan? In terms of preparation, how do you explain to students and staff the purpose of an emergency drill and make sure they are not only attentive during these drills but also not triggered or scared by them? In looking at the Incident Command Structure of your crisis response plan, make sure that protocols are in place to manage the mental and emotional response to a crisis, and to the toll these kinds of crises take on first responders, teachers, and administrators. After the crisis is over, you also need to include how the team will debrief the response and determine how to support the psychological well-being of everyone who experienced the crisis. From a mental health perspective, this includes the trauma response that may impact students and adults for days, weeks, and months after the event.

PAUSE AND REFLECT

Take a moment to think, discuss, or write about these questions:

1. What is your crisis response plan?

2. Does it explicitly address mental health issues and how to manage them during and after a crisis?

3. How often do key stakeholders in your school and community practice the plan?

CONCLUDING THOUGHTS

Every day, some of our students and fellow educators are struggling with mental health or some form of mental illness. This is not a new phenomenon. What is different today is that we are (thankfully) more aware and open to discussing mental illness. And we have much better ways of offering support. Yet these Tier 3 issues remain the most difficult for us to manage because they are really, really hard, even more so when the people grappling with them are children or adolescents. Yes, in some cases, this could be a matter of life or death. This means we must create systems that will reduce the number and then offer the highest quality intervention and recovery support possible.

In this chapter, we've taken a closer look at multiple serious mental health challenges and mental illnesses. As a school leader, you must have some knowledge about the broad spectrum of mental health challenges so you know the signs and know a little bit about treatment. This will allow you to be better able to create Tier 3 support systems, respond to crises, and hire the best mental health professionals to work in your school. You also need to make sure that everyone in the school or district or organization you lead knows the signs of mental illness and what the protocol is for getting that student or colleague the help they need. It should also be apparent that your Tier 3 intervention and response systems must be led by highly qualified educators, social workers, psychologists, and nurses. They are critically important and should be supported with additional training and learning so they stay current on evidence-based practices. You also should avail yourself of every resource in the local, state, and federal community to bring even more help to your students and staff.

A comprehensive mental health action plan includes prevention and intervention systems at all three levels of a Multi-Tiered System of Support. These work in concert with each other to provide a continuum of care, like a safety net, for every individual and for every situation. Not every person is going to need Tier 3 support but we need to build a system where every person could use it. In our experience, when Tiers 1 and 2 are thoughtfully designed and implemented, the number of people needing Tier 3 support becomes quite small and allows us to bring all our resources to bear on their behalf. Now is the time to build those systems so your school is proactive rather than reactive, yet flexible and creative to respond to whatever new challenges face us in the future.

CREATING YOUR MENTAL HEALTH ACTION PLAN

Take some time to work with your school-based team to think through the following elements of your comprehensive Mental Health Action Plan. The full plan template is located in Appendix A.

Prevention and Intervention Plan: Tier 3

1. Do we have suicide prevention, intervention and postvention plans, procedures, and policies?

2. What information and resources do we rely on related to more severe mental illnesses, such as depression, nonsuicidal non-injury, eating disorders, suicidal ideation, and adverse childhood trauma?

3. What prevention and interventions do we engage in to support students and staff who are grappling with Tier 3 issues?

4. How do we deal with stigma related to serious mental health issues?

Crisis Response Plan

Crisis plans are living documents and crisis management is a continuous process. A good plan is never finished:

1. What is our crisis response plan?

2. Where is it stored?

3. Do we regularly edit and practice it? If yes, how often? If no, what are the barriers?

4. What are its strengths and weaknesses?

5. Who is on our crisis team and are the roles and tasks clearly defined?

REFERENCES

American Psychiatric Association. (2013). *Diagnostic and statistical manual of mental disorders* (5th ed.). https://doi.org/10.1176/appi.books.9780890425596

Burke Harris, N. (2018). *The deepest well: Healing the long-term effects of childhood adversity.* Houghton Mifflin Harcourt.

Centers for Disease Control and Prevention. (2023a). *Youth risk behavior surveillance system.* https://www.cdc.gov/healthyyouth/data/yrbs/index.htm

Centers for Disease Control and Prevention. (2023b). *Adverse childhood experiences.* https://www.cdc.gov/violenceprevention/aces/index.html

Craig, S. E. (2016). *Trauma-sensitive schools: Learning communities transforming children's lives, K–5.* Teachers College Press.

Erbacher, T. A., Singer, J. B., & Poland, S. (2015). *Comprehensive case study. Suicide in schools: A practitioner's guide to multi-level prevention, assessment, intervention and postvention.* Routledge.

Erika's Lighthouse. (2023). www.erikaslighthouse.org

Evans, S. W., Petca, A. R., & Owens, J. S. (2015). Treating children and adolescents with attention deficit hyperactivity disorder in the schools. In K. Corcoran & A. R. Roberts (Eds.), *Social worker's desk reference* (3rd ed., pp. 1079–1087). Oxford University Press.

Hauber, K., Boon, A., & Vermeiren, R. (2019). Non-suicidal self-injury in clinical practice. *Frontiers in Psychology, 10,* 502. https://doi.org/10.3389/fpsyg.2019.00502

Jennings, P. (2018). *The trauma-sensitive classroom: Building resilience with compassionate teaching.* Norton.

Karatekin, C., & Hill, M. (2018, November 12). Expanding the original definition of adverse childhood experiences (ACEs). *Journal of Child & Adolescent Trauma, 12*(3), 289–306. https://doi.org/10.1007/s40653-018-0237-5

Klonsky, E. D., Victor, S. E., & Saffer, B. Y. (2014). Nonsuicidal self-injury: What we know, and what we need to know. *Canadian Journal of Psychiatry, 59*(11), 565–568. https://doi.org/10.1177/070674371405901101.

National Alliance on Mental Illness. (2023). *Mental health by the numbers.* https://www.nami.org/mhstats.

National Association of Anorexia NervosaAssociated Disorders. (2023). *Eating disorder awareness and education.* https://www.eatingdisorderhope.com/information.

National Institute on Drug Abuse. (2022, December 15). *Most reported substance use among adolescents held steady in 2022.* https://nida.nih.gov/news-events/news-releases/2022/12/most-reported-substance-use-among-adolescents-held-steady-in-2022.

National Institute of Mental Health. (2023). *Suicide.* https://www.nimh.nih.gov/health/statistics/suicide.

National Institute of Mental Health. (n.d.). *Major depression.* https://www.nimh.nih.gov/health/statistics/major-depression.

Odgers, C. L., Caspi, A., Nagin, D. S., Piquero, A. R., Slutske, W. S., Milne, B. J., Dickson, N., Poulton, R., & Moffitt, T. E. (2008). Is it important to prevent early exposure to drugs and alcohol among adolescents? *Psychological Science, 19*(10), 1037–1044. https://doi.org/10.1111/j.1467-9280.2008.02196.x.

Rathus, J., Berk, M., Miller, A., & Halpert, R. (2020). Dialectical behavior therapy for adolescents: A review of the research. In J. Bedics (Ed.), *The handbook of dialectical behavior therapy*. Academic Press.

Rathus, J., Miller, A., & Lineham, M. (2014). *DBT skills manual for adolescents*. Guilford Press.

Romero, V., Robertson, R., & Warner, A. (2018). *Building resilience in students impacted by adverse childhood experiences: A whole-staff approach*. Corwin.

Singer, J. B., & McManama O'Brien, K. H. (2015). Assessment, prevention and intervention with suicidal youth. In K. Corcoran & A. R. Roberts (Eds.), *Social workers' desk reference* (3rd ed., pp. 516–528). Oxford University Press.

Stobbe, M. (2023, August 10). *U.S. suicides hit an all-time high last year*. Associated Press. https://apnews.com/article/suicides-record-2022-guns-48511d74deb24d933e66cec1b6f2d545

Substance Abuse and Mental Health Services Administration. (2023). *Behavioral health equity*. https://www.samhsa.gov/behavioral-health-equity

Venet, A. S. (2023). *Equity-centered trauma-informed education*. Routledge.

CHAPTER 6

....

INTEGRATING THE MENTAL HEALTH ACTION PLAN IN YOUR SCHOOL

The fact is that given the challenges we face, education doesn't need to be reformed— it needs to be transformed. The key to this transformation is not to standardize education, but to personalize it, to build achievement on discovering the individual talents of each child, to put students in an environment where they want to learn and where they can naturally discover their true passions.

—Sir Ken Robinson

When Tim went from a classroom teacher to principal of a large high school, he quickly realized that the school was a big, complex system. After years of thinking only about his own classroom and students and himself, he suddenly saw how everything in the school connected to everything else, that he was part of a much larger system of interconnected parts. This view of the world is called "systems thinking" and it is one of the most important new skills school leaders must learn if they are going to be successful (Fullan, 2006; Senge, 2006). It is the ability to hold two things in your thinking at once: the individual parts and the whole, the forest and the trees. It is also the key to enacting a comprehensive Mental Health Action Plan in your school.

This chapter is all about the word *comprehensive*. It is what Harvard's David Perkins calls "playing the whole game" (2009). Just like in any sport, there are essential skills and knowledge we must master on our own but at some point we need to bring them all together into a coherent whole and use them to play the actual game. In baseball, this means hitting, throwing, fielding, and running eventually get translated into a nine-inning game. In schools, it means everything students experience in the course of a school day from the trip to school to the classroom to the hallways to the cafeteria to after-school activities to arriving home at the end of the day make up the total student experience.

So far, we've looked at the important mental models that should undergird our approach to mental health. We've looked at context and the various mental health challenges facing kids and adults, as well as some ways in an MTSS system that teachers and leaders can prevent or intervene on those challenges. Now we want to look broadly across the entire school system for ways we can more deeply integrate mental health into all aspects of a school.

BEGIN WITH BELONGING

Belonging is about connection and it is a good place to start thinking about how to make your school mentally healthy from the inside out. It's about being seen and valued as an individual and as a member of a larger community. Belonging is more than just a feeling. It's the lived experience of engagement, and engagement in context, in a community. A community of care and engagement results in connection, relationships, and that sense of belonging. When communities are fractured or isolated or when communities are grappling with toxic issues that threaten rather than build connection and safety, mental health can be threatened profoundly. Those deep relationships have been shown to improve resilience, recover after a loss, and increase student achievement. Educator James Comer said, "No significant learning takes place without a significant relationship."

Skills that are central to engagement are empathy, noticing, listening, and care. There is an intricate relationship between engagement and teaching and learning. When we are known and when students are invited into relationships we build trust, confidence and creativity. We also can provide support at those moments when somebody is struggling with a mental health issue like loss, grief, sadness, or trauma. Engagement is an emotional investment or commitment. In our classrooms, it's a process of building relationships, creating an environment of care, genuine empathy, and warmth. It's forming learning partnerships and establishing a basis for trust and community. Engagement is both an intentional process and a commitment to creating a space where learning takes place. But the key aspect of relationships is that of feeling engaged being seen, known, and valued.

One of the earliest school shootings occurred in Winnetka, Illinois, in 1988 at an elementary school. The principal of that school, Dick Streedain, navigated the entire school and community through this horrific tragedy and recognized how belonging and a community of care are necessary to emerge from a crisis. Streedain describes the essential requirements of such a school: "When kids have an adult who really know them, when they process things together as a group, live John's Dewey's principles teaching to the whole child, where teachers always connect to their students or students are supported intellectually emotionally, socially. . . where moral, ethical, spiritual, and physical needs are addressed. I think we were really living that philosophy. So the healthier you are going into [a crisis], the healthier the recovery is going to be" (Personal communication, August 23, 2023). Belonging is essential to surviving even the most terrible tragedies. And it is something more school leaders need to prioritize in their schools.

RETHINKING THE ORGANIZATION OF A SCHOOL

If we apply a mental health "lens" to thinking about schools, we might want to look at the very organization of the school. This includes multiple aspects of our schools, including how they are built, use of time, staffing, curriculum, instruction, assessment, and outreach. Some of these aspects are left over from previous decades or even centuries in response to issues that are no longer relevant at best or detrimental to mental health at worst. Teachers and administrators today find themselves at odds with these past decisions all the time, including onerous and unfair grading practices, punitive discipline, buildings built to look like prisons or factories, classrooms built for lectures only, or systems built around "seat time" rather than learning. If we were to build a school from scratch today using everything we know about mental health, the brain, learning, and human development . . . how would we design and organize the school?

One of the systems educators have the most control over is time, yet we often feel as if past practices and other forces leave us with no other options. Unfortunately, the way schools traditionally use time is mired in 19th-century or 20th-century decisions that are not reflective of modern society, the workplace, or what we know from research. We apply "credit" for "seat time" and Carnegie Units, which are all supposed to quantify what a student has learned. This has led us down a path of determining school schedules that are tied to these systems and led to a hypersegmented experience for both students and teachers. Instead of allowing student experience learning a topic or teacher expertise to determine how long we spend on something that day or over several days, we force them to move too quickly or linger too long on certain aspects of the curriculum. Or we decide that math will always be learned in the morning and language arts in the afternoon. These kinds of decisions based on schedules and past practices separates the learner from learning and can cause a tremendous amount of stress and anxiety in everyone from elementary students learning how to read up to high school students learning U.S. history.

The recent COVID-19 pandemic forced many schools to change schedules to accommodate remote learning and smaller class sizes for social distancing. Some had students learn in shifts while others experimented with block schedules. These kinds of innovations, which had previously been used in a small number of schools, have opened the door for school administrations to feel more comfortable moving away from past practices and allowing school schedules to support both academics and student mental health. This can also benefit teachers and staff by giving them reasonable breaks to decompress and time to collaborate with colleagues, hold meetings, or engage in professional learning. What is the best length of a learning segment from both an academic and mental health perspective? How might elementary, middle, or high school students benefit from shorter or longer segments? What impact does movement or mindful moments have on learning and engagement?

Another way we should use time differently from a mental health perspective relates to start times for students. We previously discussed the importance of sleep in child development and in adults. This is especially true for adolescents whose circadian rhythm works best with a slightly later start time than is traditional in schools. The American Academy of Pediatrics and the Centers for Disease Control both recommend that middle and high schools should start their day at 8:30 a.m. or later (CDC, 2022; Owens et al., 2014). In order to support student mental health, more and more schools are following this recommendation and pushing their start times to 9 a.m. or even later. In 2019, California passed a law mandating all high schools had to start school no earlier than 8 a.m. and other states are following their lead, as are some large school districts such as Denver and Philadelphia (Schultz, 2023). Schools would also be wise to educate children and adults about the importance of sleep on physical and mental health to make sure everyone is getting the sleep they need to be at their best.

The schedule of the week and year should also be reconsidered in light of its impact on mental health. Some schools have moved to four days of school per week which can allow for more time with families or pursuing activities outside school hours. It can also provide teachers with valuable planning and professional development time. Some schools have moved to or experimented with year-round school schedules, breaking away from the traditional 180-day calendar from August to June. The benefits of more evenly spacing out breaks between semesters include reducing the potential "learning loss" of a long summer break but also providing students with a much more regular school year calendar of semesters punctuated with short breaks between them.

Other schools have taken a close look at the compressed nature of their calendars and stretched it out longer to ensure all students can fully enjoy civic and religious holidays, as well as more regular long weekends as ways of having some downtime during the academic year. Other schools have moved the start of their school year earlier in order to end a semester just before December and January holidays so students can take a real break from school. All of these can potentially benefit students and staff by reducing stress and increasing opportunities for downtime, play, relationship-building, and engaging in family activities.

RETHINKING THE PHYSICAL BUILDING

A school building itself can have either positive or negative effects on the mental health of the people who learn and work there. Usually administrators and physical plant services are the only ones thinking about the building, but there is so much we can due to improve mental health through the facilities. While we don't often have the chance to impact the design of a school building, there are times when communities build or renovate schools so it is a great chance to rethink them in light of mental and physical health.

This starts with the front door! School entrances and exits have become a source of great scrutiny over the past 20 years as school violence has become more of a threat. While we have tried to make our schools safer, we have also made it more difficult to feel welcomed at the schoolhouse gate. During student arrival and dismissal, students and families should be welcomed to the school by staff located outside the school. Seeing smiling administrators, teachers, and staff in the parking lots, traffic circles, and outside the school door can greatly reduce anxiety and be a first signal of that culture of caring we are trying to create. Once the school day has begun, clear and welcoming signage at school doors plus friendly protocols for visitors can also help parents and others feel welcomed but still maintain safety procedures. We know principals and administrators who also walk the neighborhood at different times during the school day to be more aware of how school operations are impacting the community. It is also a great opportunity to build better relationships with neighbors.

Over the past 20 years, we've also started to pay more attention to how the physical environment of the school building and classrooms impact student learning and student mental health. From an environmental point of view, air quality, lighting, sound, flooring materials, and access to the outdoors can either distract from or improve learning (Filardo et al., 2019; Schneider, 2002). Many studies have now shown evidence of how these school design and environmental factors can raise test scores and academic achievement.

There are also other studies that point to the positive impact on mental and emotional health when students and staff are surrounded by clean air, sunlight, and moderate temperature and sound. Access to green space, the outdoors, or even the ability to see these through windows can also help students and staff reduce stress and remain positive (Moser, 2016). Researchers, like Dr. Theresa Horton at Northwestern University, are finding links between nature and cortisol and glucose levels, and even aging (Browning & Rigolon, 2019; Horton, 2021; Paul, 2023). This means that adding more plants, lawns, raised planting beds, or rooftop gardens can help everyone feel better and potentially learn more, as can regular walks outside during the school day.

In the classroom, there are many ways teachers, staff, and administrators can improve the environment to help students feel comfortable and better engage in learning. In creating a trauma-informed classroom, teachers can think about how lighting, sound, and temperature might impact a student. Harsh fluorescent lights can be covered by a diffuser or fabric to soften the light shining down on students. While some students might be energized by music being played as they enter class, others may be distracted or triggered by it so monitor sound levels carefully and talk to kids about what makes them feel comfortable. Teachers should also think about students who may have hearing disabilities and ask their administration to purchase microphone and speaker systems to amplify teacher and student voices.

Classroom furniture that is flexible and comfortable, especially furniture that can flex or bounce a little, can provide students with the right amount of movement to keep them focused and engaged. Many elementary teachers have moved away from rows of desks and created stations and areas where the furniture is more appropriate for the activity, such as water tables, bean bags chairs, or small tables for collaboration. It is also quite common to see calming corners or calming chairs in classrooms at all grade levels, which are wonderful places where students can choose to sit and regulate themselves when they are stressed or anxious. Often, teachers will add fidget spinners, coloring books, or puzzles to these spaces.

In many school climate surveys and research we've conducted over decades, a common pattern regarding student feelings of safety is that most will say they feel safe in their classrooms but not so much in other areas of a school. These non-classroom spaces are often also more informal student spaces with less direct teacher or staff supervision, such as hallways, bathrooms, locker rooms, cafeterias, playgrounds, and parking lots. Some schools have utilized camera systems to better monitor these areas but these are not useful at the moment of an incident and can add an element of "big brother" watching students, leading to distrust. Administrators need to create staffing plans for supervising these areas or securing them so students can't access them without supervision. We've also learned that these are also spaces where staff must be carefully trained to manage students and build positive relationships and environments where all kids feel safe.

In one school we worked with, school climate surveys showed very negative feelings of the students toward security staff, who were most visible in hallways, study halls, and the cafeteria. We spent a day observing these areas and discovered the reason for this response. When the bell for the passing period rang and students moved into the hallways, security staff often yelled at groups of students: "Keep moving!" "Get to class!" "Ya'll are going to be late!" In the study halls and cafeteria, security staff continued to loudly bark orders to students, chastise them for gathering in groups, or not following pretty strict rules regarding which direction to sit in a chair or for silence.

When we reported our survey results, observations and some video of what had become normal, daily interactions, school leaders saw clearly that the positive climate their teachers created in classrooms was forgotten upon stepping into the hallway. The following week, the assistant principal led groups of the security staff through some retraining and role-play. There was an immediate change in the noise level in the hallways and student complaints about security staff diminished. By the following fall, after making some personnel decisions and additional training, with a focus on development connections with kids, students began reporting that the security staff were among their favorite adults in the school.

RETHINKING TECHNOLOGY AND MENTAL HEALTH

One of the most common questions we field from both educators and parents is about technology and screen time. What role does technology play on mental health? New technologies have always found a way to change our society and culture, sometimes with both significant benefits and problems. Certainly, educational technology has helped millions of students for decades to access information more easily and for teachers to improve instruction, whether that was film, video, computers, or software. We want to continue using technology in schools to improve access and deepen learning.

The difference today is that mobile technology in the form of a phone, laptop, or tablet is more ubiquitous than ever, both in school and at home. This raises a concern about screen time as both young and older students may find themselves in front of a screen both during and after school. Medical experts agree that young people should limit the amount of time they spend in front of screens as it can lead to isolation, distraction, sleeplessness, and obesity (Ruder, 2019). According to The American Academy of Pediatrics, children younger than two should not be exposed to screens and elementary-age children should be limited to no more than one to two hours of screen time per day (Mayo Clinic System, 2021). Anything we can due to put parameters around total screen time will help reduce problems when young people are grappling with other mental health issues.

What may be more important is what is happening on those screens. Social media has the potential to connect people in positive ways, especially ado-lescents and young adults who are yearning for social connection and creating peer groups around similar interests. However, there is growing concern that social media applications and software may have an overall negative effect on mental health. Evidence is mounting that social media is leading to increased problems such as sleep loss, relational difficulties with family and or peers, preoccupations that lead to anxiety, lower self-esteem, a lack of in-person social connectedness, feelings of exclusion, isolation, and possible victimiza-tion (West, 2023).

Social media is a risk factor that may exacerbate mental health issues as they relate to anxiety, depression, and addictive disorders. Questions to consider include, What role does social media play in the student's adjustment and functioning? How does social media promote adaptive behavior? How does it interfere with prosocial functioning? Students who are drawn toward impulsivity, have difficulty with attention, or who are struggling with relationships or loneliness may be at greater risk and negatively impacted by social media. As with any intervention, assessment is essential in order to determine what to do and how to do it. Adults working with a student struggling with social media issues should consider the scope, depth, and range of social media engagement. As always, a coordinated effort at school and at home will be necessary to provide the appropriate intervention.

So, if we were to rethink our schools and technology usage from a mental health perspective, what might we do differently? Educators need to be more clear with students and parents about the use of technology in schools for learning. These are powerful tools for kids and we need to explain how they enhance learning and their role in teaching and learning through information access, producing examples of student learning, authentic assessment, collaboration, and communication. We can also educate students about the best ways to use technology ethically and safely, both in school and in life. Knowing how technology is being used and taught in school means parents can supplement this at home and help guide young people in the best ways to manage technology. CommonSense.org is a great resource for educators and parents to think through some of these ideas which are commonly referred to as "digital citizenship."

RETHINKING CURRICULUM, INSTRUCTION, AND ASSESSMENT

Mental health and well-being have become critical elements of recent research on the science of learning. When we talk about overall school climate, we are talking about the academic, social, emotional, and physical elements of the classroom and school. They all have an impact on engagement, growth, and achievement. A report from the Learning Policy Institute and Turnaround for Children in 2021 called "Design Principles for Schools" laid out the most recent research on how students learn best and connected it to many of the mental health and wellness issues we've explored in this book. Using the latest research about learning and development, they show that to create engaging, positive, and healthy classrooms and schools for kids we must address both cognition and mental health. At the core of what we do in classrooms is curriculum, instruction, and assessment. Let's take a closer look at how some teachers are rethinking these in light of mental health.

In its most basic form, curriculum is the content of what students learn, which means just about everything they see, hear, or experience is part of the curriculum. When we ask kids or adults about what they learned in school it is often more than what was in the textbook but rather how people treated them or a memory of an event, both good or bad, so we need to pay attention to not just the content of a written curriculum but also overall experiences. From the lens of diversity, it is essential that students can see themselves represented in the curriculum. This means doing regular curriculum audits for gaps in the representation of different voices and points of view, including race, class, gender, ability, ideology, and so on. The curriculum should also go beyond technical or historical knowledge to include material that is inspiring, compelling, or emotional. Skills should certainly be built around academic knowledge but they should also focus on communication, social and emotional learning, and physical wellness. Ethics and decision-making should be a central part of the curriculum, as should self-care and managing emotions.

RETHINKING TEACHERS AND INSTRUCTION

As we dig into the intersection of mental health and classroom instruction, the most powerful force is the teacher. Study after study shows that teacher effectiveness impacts student learning but also student experience (Jackson et al., 2014). This is the greatest investment school leaders can make, so for a moment, let's consider how teachers should be supported in a mentally healthy school. This starts with recruitment and hiring. Teachers should reflect the demographics of the students in front of them. However, the teaching force across the United States is still predominantly white and female. While this is slowly changing, school leaders must make recruiting diverse teachers a priority by looking within the community and well beyond it.

"Grow your own" recruitment and teacher training is emerging as an important approach that takes community members and current non-licensed staff members and offers them the chance to take licensure coursework while working with kids as paraprofessionals and classroom aides. Some districts are investing in current students by offering courses and clubs on teaching, using them as peer mentors for other students and also teaching them about education in hopes that they go on to major in education in college. Organizations like the Golden Apple Foundation (www.goldenapple.org) even offer scholarships and training for high school and college students who promise to return to their community to teach. School leaders can also use national job boards and websites to recruit teachers from other parts of the country or the world to diversify their teaching force and find high-quality teachers.

Once we hire them, it is imperative that schools begin to invest in teachers and support them on their journey through the profession. Ultimately, this will result in more effective teachers who stay in their schools and the profession for decades. High-quality professional development is also critical to making sure your Mental Health Action Plan is enacted with fidelity in all classrooms and throughout the school. The school's philosophy on mental health should start to be communicated in recruitment materials, throughout the hiring process, and into new teacher orientation and induction. Experienced and trained mentors should work with novice teachers on improving their classroom instruction but also how to develop relationships with students and enact a continuum of care.

Instructional coaching has been shown to not only improve learning with teachers of all experience levels but also improve student experience and overall morale of the staff (Knight, 2013). Teachers who are competent and trained in the latest and most effective research-based instructional approaches and human development feel more confident in their teaching abilities, allowing them to not only positively impact student learning but also stay in the profession for a long time. Schools should also look for ways to give teachers opportunities to lead their schools and grow as teacher leaders. All of these things help support positive morale and fend off burnout. School climate is just as important for teachers as it is for students. We must think about the cognitive, social, emotional and physical well-being of our teachers, too.

As teachers and leaders, we tend to focus on the teaching rather than the learning, which means we focus on teachers rather than students. In a mentally healthy school, learning is all about the students. This is called a *student-centered classroom*. It starts with building a relationship with kids and understanding who they are and where they come from. We need to hire and nurture teachers who are intensely curious about kids.

A student-centered classroom also puts the focus on kids during instruction. Certainly, there are important moments when a teacher needs to lecture or do a demonstration or explicitly teach a skill, but these should be the exception and not the rule. Students must be given the opportunity to grapple with problems, explore ideas, work collaboratively, and engage in safe and appropriate "productive struggle" to understand themselves, each other, and the world around them (Hammond, 2015). Cooperative learning strategies like Think-Pair-Share and jigsaws place students as "thought partners" and "investigators" on problems that not only engage them cognitively but also socially and emotionally. Project-based learning is another powerful strategy that is authentic, student-generated learning that teaches a broad range of both academic, social, and emotional skills, especially problem-solving and cooperation. Service learning goes beyond community service to help students understand the history and reasons behind the service work. Students don't just work in a soup kitchen or food bank, they study why poverty occurs and ways of solving the problem. Student-centered learning allows students to bring their whole selves to the classroom and engage in a way that is safe, compelling, and personalized.

RETHINKING ASSESSMENT

This same approach should be used when designing classroom assessments. In today's schools, assessment has become a negative word when, in fact, it is an essential part of the classroom. While standardized tests can be useful tools in understanding large-scale progress at the national, state, and district level, it is relatively unhelpful for students and teachers on a day-to-day basis. And at its worst, a hyperfixation on standardized test scores can result in unnecessary stress and anxiety for students, teachers, and parents.

In a mentally healthy school and classroom, assessment is authentic, formative, and student centered. It is what Rick Stiggins calls "assessment FOR learning" (2024), which is simply assessment that helps students and teachers identify what a student knows and where to go next in their learning. Every class session, students should ask themselves what they know and what they don't know, what they want to learn next, and what could I due to get there? Simple activities like entry and exit tickets, self-assessments, and nonscored quizzes can provide that daily feedback to students and teachers to answer those questions. Project-based learning, investigations, and portfolios offer deeper dives into what students have learned while also giving them the chance to reflect on their learning and share it with the teacher and others. In a mentally healthy classroom, assessment is a feedback loop to students and teachers about progress and understanding that should drive curriculum, instruction, and learning.

Unfortunately, assigning grades to school work and courses has become one of the most mentally unhealthy activities in our schools. In fact, we seem to have lost all sight of the purpose of grades. There is some benefit for us to look at the quality of our work in relation to our past work or a standard we are trying to meet or even sometimes in comparison to others. This is true in life and in schooling. In being explicit about that evaluation of our work, we use tools like rubrics and standards to explain where the work stands in that comparison. Over time, we have created a shorthand for that explanation that results in descriptors like "excellent," "proficient," and "poor," or grade levels like A, B, C. In standardized tests, we use even less descriptive terms like the number on a scale, like a 1,200 out of 1,600. All of this is a kind of "feedback" to students but because we have boiled it down to a single word or number or letter, it loses its ability to describe nuance and depth and complexity of the work or of the person.

A student-centered, mentally healthy grading system returns us to a system that uses thick, descriptive feedback on our work that is useful in seeing what we have done well and where we need to get better. Formative assessment relies on written or verbal feedback that is embedded in the work and offers the student a chance to have a conversation about it so they can really learn from it. On the end of term report cards, we will see sentences and paragraphs offering that summative feedback, instead of a single piece of paper with letters or numbers. All of this rejects the current kinds of grading practices that are reductive, unfair, inequitable, and often grade students for behavior as much as for learning (Feldman, 2019). Assessment and grading must be student centered if they are going to positively support mental health.

RETHINKING TRANSITIONS

Transitions are the process of experiencing change. Some are abrupt. Some are developmental. Some are seasonal. Some are small and we take them for granted, like a passing period or a shift from one activity to another in a classroom lesson. There are transitions upon entering and there are transitions when we leave. With any transition, there is a beginning, a middle, and an end. We are experiencing a change in both our identity and experience. Think about this: What does it feel like to start at a new school or walk into a new classroom of peers? Or a cafeteria? Is it safe? Is it comfortable? Too often schools don't consider the many transitions our students experience, let alone plan how to manage them with mental health in mind. How mindful and attentive are we to these? What are the emotional experiences? What are the social experiences? How do you "mark" or recognize a transition?

Because we are experiencing a change during a transition means there is a great deal of stress and anxiety connected with it. As with any issue, we must first recognize and be aware of the transition as a moment of change. This includes awareness of how you are reacting and responding to the transition. How are you managing your emotions and body? Are you reaching out to other people for support and to make a connection? Is this similar or different from past transitions? We must engage our problem-solving skills to manage the transition and prepare for future transitions. If we don't manage these transitions well, we can cause more problems, including high levels of stress, potential overload, and even burnout. The brain may be on high-alert and not able to process information well. It is important to stay present in the moment, self-reflect on what is happening, and make good decisions.

Schools can do much to support students and staff in managing transitions. This can start by being aware of transitions that are occurring and how they may be affecting students. Teachers and staff can do an inventory of all the different transitions and ask how well we are doing in helping students manage them. Know your students well enough to meet and greet them to create a sense of belonging and recognize when one of them might be struggling with a transition. Stand outside the classroom or school to meet and greet students. On a recent school visit, we watched Mrs. Jorgenson stand outside the school doors before the day started to personally greet each second grader in her class and make a personal connection by welcoming each by name, asking about something happening last night, or commenting on their cool shoes or backpack. Her familiar, friendly face helped students connect with the school as they said good-bye to a parent or caregiver. It also gave her a chance to start the process of orienting them to the school day and today's lessons.

The passing periods between classes or sessions can be triggering to some students. Even a bell system that rings can negatively impact students. Some schools play music during passing periods, which can be calming or energizing for some kids but negative to others. As class begins, teachers should pay attention to the transition and create a "landing space" for students. For example, some teachers will call for a "Mindful Moment" at the start of a class session or at the end as a transition in or out of the session. Immediately writing for a few minutes in a journal can serve the same function, as can an entry ticket or exit ticket with a math problem or compelling question to ponder. When combined with formative assessments, not only does the teacher support their transition but they also receive useful instructional feedback to utilize immediately or the next day.

These same kinds of activities can be used when students are moving from one activity or lesson to the next. Being able to pause before or after an activity engages them in valuable self-reflection while focusing them on the next task, such as starting the rotation on a series of learning stations or beginning a science lab or moving into small group projects. We can also use transitions as a way to manage student behavior or support students who might be struggling. Many schools use daily check ins and check outs with specific students who need to make individual contact with an adult in the building to stay on task or to reinforce positive behavior.

Outside the classroom, schools can support students, families, and staff by focusing on moments of transition. When new students and families move into the district, the transition to the new school can be stressful. Schools can identify a staff member to be the liaison for new families as they fill out paperwork, gather the correct school supplies, and answer their questions. As students and families move from one school building in the district to a new one, there should be orientation activities that begin in the previous school year and continue into the new school year. Older students can give tours of the new building to new students and families. After the year has started, teachers and staff should contact home to see how the student is managing the transition and to see if they have any questions.

We also need to see long weekends, holidays, or vacations as moments of transition that can be both energizing but also disruptive. We have previously discussed the impact of an extended illness or hospitalization and our need to help provide a soft "landing pad" for students coming back to school after them. Endings are another transition we should consider, like the end of a school year or matriculating to a different school building or seniors graduating from high school. Or staff who are retiring or leaving the job. We should celebrate the past but also recognize that there is some loss occurring and there may be a need to work through a kind of mourning at this change. Ceremonies marking this kind of transition like graduations, recognition ceremonies, or parties are important. Some schools also engage students and staff who are leaving in exit interviews to not only learn about ways of improving the organization but also giving the outgoing person a chance to have a final say. All these kinds of transition impacts teachers and staff as well! We must pay attention to how they are experiencing a new school and job so we can reduce their stress.

One powerful school structure we can implement to help support the overall mental health action plan are morning meetings and advisories. These structures, usually at the start of the day in elementary, middle, or high schools, give students and teachers a chance to be with a small community as the school day begins. As a transition, it signals to students that learning is starting. It also provides the teacher with an opportunity to check in with individuals and the entire group in order to make any adjustments to the schedule or lesson plan. Since the teacher and students know each other well in these groups, it deepens the culture of caring and collaboration between students and the teacher. Some schools implement a curriculum in these sessions, often related to social and emotional learning but they can also delve into study strategies, academics, diversity, equity, inclusion, college and career, guest speakers, and school culture.

In middle schools and high schools, where students move between classrooms and teachers, an advisory becomes a constant community for connection and communication. Sometimes the same group and advisor stay together throughout their time in a school building. At one high school, the advisor and group are together for all four years and at graduation the advisor is the one who gives the student their diploma. If there is a need to have a difficult conversation or deliver sensitive information to students, an advisory can be a perfect place to do this, leveraging the trusting relationship with the advisor and the camaraderie of the advisory.

RETHINKING AFTER-SCHOOL ACTIVITIES

The life of a student (or staff) doesn't end when the final bell rings. After-school activities, whether sponsored by the school or not, can have a massive impact on school attendance, learning, and mental health. Sometimes these activities, not school, are the reasons a student gets up in the morning. These activities can provide social connection, deep learning on topics of interest, a sense of success and accomplishment, fun and enjoyment (AIR, 2015). Most are not graded nor do they carry as much stress and anxiety as academic achievement. And the informal nature of some activities can also create a loose environment that can feel relaxing.

Since many of these activities are sponsored by a school or organization, it also places students in contact with adult supervisors, which means the hiring and training of those adults is key, especially in managing the mental and physical health of young people. According to the Afterschool Alliance, almost eight million children participate in after-school programs, with elementary age children accounting for 60% of those kids (2020). Clearly, this is an area that calls for attention in your Mental Health Action Plan.

Many elementary, middle, and high schools offer before or after-school activities. These can include clubs, athletics, fine arts, performing arts, or service learning. Student clubs can bring students together around specific topics like anime, cooking, games, or diversity.

They can be academic topics like science, math, business, or academic honors societies. A wide variety of clubs can provide a community and connection for students that requires a low investment in time and space. Fine and per- forming arts activities, like newspaper, yearbook, creative writing, drama, debate, or art, allow students to explore their creative sides and often produce works that can be enjoyed by other students and the community. Competitive and noncompetitive athletics programs not only teach physical skills but can also be important ways to learn social and emotional skills like self-awareness, team-building, and decision-making. Don't forget to include wellness and leisure activities such as weight-lifting, hiking, or rock-climbing.

Many schools offer opportunities for students to engage in community service. Some even require it for graduation. Service learning goes beyond community service by also teaching students about the history and issues surrounding that service. For example, students may study invasive species and then go to a local forest preserve to clear buckthorn and other invasive plants. Or they may learn about child development and literacy then go to a local preschool school to read with children. Service learning is one of the best ways for a student to practice all the various social and emotional skills, which can then help strengthen their own mental health.

Schools should also recognize the many activities students engage in outside formal schooling that impact mental health and wellness. In doing so, educators may make different decisions about things like homework or to give students credit for the good work they are doing in the community. Students may be working a job to make money for themselves or for their families. Some of them may be care-giving for children at a very young age, or helping with an elderly relative or neighbor. Others might spend their time volunteering at local agencies or organizations helping others. There can be organizations in the community that provide a space and activities for students after school, like the YMCA, libraries, park district programs, or social service agencies. School leaders should reach out to these groups to see how they can coordinate resources to support students as they engage in these activities.

There is a growing body of research about outside-of-school learning and the role it plays in overall growth and development, as well as school achievement (McCombs et al., 2017). Schools need to see the impact of these programs. Many students find their religious life to be a core part of their identity and invest out of school time in these communities. Of course, students will also spend time learning on their own, through reading, writing, art, and exploration. Or they may find informal social life to be a motivator. Friends and family are essential relationships that not only help build resilience and offer support in times of need, but they also are another way for kids to learn about various academic topics and the world.

RETHINKING SCHOOL CONTEXT AND COMMUNITY ASSETS

In taking an ecological systems approach to schools, we have already talked several times about the importance of understanding and leveraging the context of your school, the world around you, and your students. This means being honest about what strengths and challenges, risks and protective factors exist in your community that might impact the mental health of kids, parents, and staff. For example, an elementary school in an urban neighborhood may be a centerpiece of community activity and pride yet carjacking and gunfire have become more common. In a rural school district, most of the staff attended the school themselves and have a lot of school spirit but as the only K–12 school in the county, there are few local organizations that can partner with you on programs or after-school activities. Bring your team together and conduct a local context "scan" to identify the assets and challenges in your community. Try to be as specific as possible and attach names of people who might be useful contacts in relation to those assets and challenges. Then reach out and start building a relationship with them to better understand the asset or challenge, and find ways of using those to build systems of support for students and staff.

Here's a specific example: One elementary school in an urban neighborhood recognized that their physical location in the neighborhood had both strengths and challenges. Families had confidence in the school, staff, and principal. It was close to many of their homes and students could walk to and from school pretty easily, especially with the help of some volunteer crossing guards. However, the building was old and sat on a very small piece of land, with almost no green space for recess, exercise, or athletics. This had a negative impact on student physical and mental health during the day. After school, there were few places where kids could go to play, hang out, or engage in organized sports.

As the principal and her staff did their context analysis, they identified all these issues and decided to try some things to improve the situation. They wrote a letter and held a meeting with district administrators to raise awareness about the state of the physical building and the lack of green space. They also met with their local alderman and park district officials about possibly partnering on a solution that would benefit the school and the community. As it turned out, a plot of land just down the street from the school was for sale. The principal and park district director proposed that the district and city purchase the land and redevelop it as a shared space for school and community recreation. During the day, the school would use it for recess and gym classes. After school on the weekdays and weekends, it would be used for both school sports and park district sports and events. After two years, everyone gathered for a ribbon cutting on the new fields and park. It was many hours of meetings and years of work, but teachers reported an immediate change in the physical and mental health of their students, something that continued for years later.

This example is an old idea that has become popular again: the Community School. Community schools have been found to be an effective way to improve student learning and student life (Oakes et al., 2017). Instead of the school being open for students and staff only from 8 a.m. to 3 p.m., the school is designed and operated as a 24/7, year-round institution that engages families, community members, and local organizations. They focus on four pillars of operation: integrated student support, expanded learning time and opportunities, family and community engagement, and collaborative leadership and practices. This looks different in each school based on the community. Some schools have become the local lending library because no other library exists. Others have opened health centers and provide vaccinations and immediate care. Playgrounds and playfields are not fenced off but are open to anyone in the neighborhood. Volunteers offer tax and legal consultation and workshops in the evening and weekends. On Sundays, the park district runs youth basketball and volleyball practices and games in the school gym.

Collaboration and communication between the school and local organizations is also a key part of a mental health support system for kids and adults. An All-School Wellness Team should not only have representation from programs within the school but also representatives from the local hospital, substance abuse program, police social worker, park district, local government youth commission, clergy, and other area preschools and schools. Many of these same individuals from the community should be part of your Community Response Network for times of crisis and should also include police, fire, and any other first responders. You may also want to contact local and state government officials and representatives who may want to be included in your crisis-response planning.

Outside of schools, there are many public and private organizations that are concerned about mental health and would be amazing partners in the school's action planning. The National Alliance on Mental Illness (NAMI) is the largest grassroots mental health organization with over six hundred local chapters. They can connect school leaders with facilitators who can bring training and workshops to staff, parents, and students. They also offer local support groups for both young people and adults. Erika's Lighthouse is another growing organization that focuses on teen depression and offers online resources, as well as local consultations and workshops for students and staff. Suicide prevention organizations like the Jed Foundation, the Ortus Foundation, Elyssa's Mission, and Mindwise Innovations provide both local and national resources and support to schools wanting to screen and educate about this Tier three topic. Some organizations may not be able to provide individual support to your Mental Health Action Plan but offer fantastic resources you should reference, including CASEL, the Urban League, the Aspen Foundation, and the Greater Good Science Center. Finally, don't forget about your local colleges and universities, which often not only have researchers eager to partner with schools but also may offer programming that could be part of your mental health plan.

With the continuing rise in mental illness and media reports about the mental health struggles of youth, especially post-COVID, more and more local, state, and federal legislators have entered the fray in trying to prevent and intervene. This has led to laws being passed and increased spending related to mental health. School leaders and educators need to become more active in speaking out at school board meetings, writing letters to legislators, and volunteering as witnesses when legislation is being drafted or passed through a governing body. Legislators need expert opinion and evidence so they can provide laws that will improve mental health in schools and communities.

A great example of this kind of activism is the passing of AnnMarie's Law in Illinois. In 2013, a girl named AnnMarie died by suicide and her parents, community members, and educators worked with state legislators to pass a law that mandated every school district adopt guidelines for suicide prevention education for both students and staff. A number of federal bills have been passed or under consideration that would improve funding and procedures related to mental health services and education about mental illness both in schools and communities. In 2022, the U.S. House of Representatives passed the REACH-ING Act, which is part of a larger Restoring Hope for Mental Health and Well-Being Act, bolstering programs that support mental health care for adults and children. "We are facing a mental health crisis in our country—a crisis that was greatly exacerbated by the COVID-19 pandemic," said Minnesota Representative Angie Craig. "These grants will ensure our communities, schools and mental health agencies are prepared to meet the challenges of this moment and that mental health resources are accessible and readily available to those who need them most." The federal government has also recently increased spending through several agencies that directly target mental health challenges and mental illness, specifically schools and mental health care providers.

IMPLEMENTING A COMPREHENSIVE MENTAL HEALTH ACTION PLAN

We believe that if a school were to prioritize mental health, it would make a huge difference in the lived experience of school for students, staff, and families. Even better, if we could build (or rebuild) a school from the bottom up through the lens of mental health, we would make very different decisions about every aspect of schooling. All and more of the ideas we have explored in this book would occur, starting with different mental models, developing a culture of care that responds to all three MTSS tiers, making classrooms student centered; connecting the school to the community around it; and centering diversity, equity, and inclusion to support every individual and the community at large. While there are rare occasions when we can start a school from scratch, most of our work in schools occurs in the rethinking and revising of our current schools. It is not an impossible task. It requires vision, courage, and effort. It may also take time. But in the midst of a mental health crisis where young people's lives are in jeopardy, we don't have any choice. It is time to transform schools into mentally healthy places.

Throughout this book, we have included essential questions for you and your school team to consider as you create your Mental Health Action Plan. The Plan needs to respond to your community's local context and the particular needs of your students, staff, and families. But there are some basic categories you should consider as you bring together your plan, including the following:

- Structures: What are the current systems, structures, and processes in your school that can help create your plan? What structures need to be created?

- Resources: What are your resources that can be brought to bear on your plan? What resources are lacking?

- Philosophy: What is your school's philosophy on teaching, learning, support, and mental health?

- Current context: What are the strengths and challenges of your school and community context?

- Prevention plan: What are you currently doing to prevent Tier 1, 2, and three issues? What could you do better to prevent mental health issues?

- Intervention plan: How do you currently respond to these issues? What gaps are there in your intervention work?

- Crisis response plan: Do you have a plan? Is it updated? Are you practicing it?

- Evaluation and feedback: How do you know your action plan is working? What is the feedback loop?

For most schools, this will require several years of planning and implementation. A self-study that involves representatives from all stakeholder groups across the school community should be the starting point, taking a critical look at the current context, resources, and structures to retain those things that are already working to support mental health. Time should be spent openly discussing and debating your philosophy, beliefs, values, and mental models. The more everyone in the school community is clear on your mission and who you are, the easier it will be to move into designing your tiers of prevention, intervention, and support. This is the core of your Mental Health Action Plan. Everything else, including your crisis response plan, should fall under the overall Mental Health Action Plan.

This is also the moment to determine how you will evaluate your plan and make changes to it over time. What are the measures you will use to know you are being successful? How do you measure whether your school is mentally healthy? Systems like school-climate data collection and evaluations by outside agencies will be useful in evaluating your Mental Health Action Plan. This can easily interface with any state or district requirements for school improvement. In this way, your plan is also how you evaluate the success of the entire school. Your plan should also be seen as a "living document," open to scrutiny and alteration as time goes on and context changes. It should be analyzed annually and updated, again involving stakeholders from across the community. This will also help ensure that everyone is still engaged in the plan and understand both the big picture and the subtle details of implementation.

Let's take a look at one example of a school that took this approach—to rethink their entire approach—and how it changed the life of one of its students.

A SCHOOL THAT IS CHANGING THE GAME: WOLCOTT COLLEGE PREP HIGH SCHOOL

In 2013, a group of educators and parents opened Wolcott College Preparatory High School, an independent school in Chicago, in hopes of rethinking a school from the ground up. It was specifically designed for helping students with learning differences find success where traditional schools had failed them. The school attracts a diverse student body from across the area and places restorative practices, social and emotional learning, and equity at the same high level of importance as content area mastery, college preparation, and career planning. Parents are seen as partners with the students and staff in charting the direction of the school.

The student-centered curriculum is designed to allow students to reach their full potential, ensuring they are well-prepared both academically and socially. A strengths-based approach means instruction is designed to individual needs, ensuring each student is appropriately challenged and engaged throughout the learning process. Teachers tailor lessons so that students are neither overwhelmed nor under stimulated—they know how to strike a balance that allows students to build both understanding and confidence.

A unique feature of the student experience is participation in the Learning Strategies course each year, which provides expert instruction from learning specialists to guide each student to discover their strengths and challenges, develop strategies to promote their own unique optimal learning techniques, and engage in designing an individualized learning plan. In contrast to deficit-based remedial approaches, Wolcott College Prep High School utilizes a strength-based approach to a rigorous curriculum. In addition to content instruction, strategies, skills, and mindset instruction are integrated into each course, while Learning Strategies teachers, the school Leadership Team, and academic coaches provide additional support. Use of all available methods to enhance learning and demonstrate progress are engaged and documentation of accommodations is maintained to support the post high school transition. Students participate in activities or sports annually, and they select from many offerings, often student initiated, to explore their interests and develop their talents, from affinity groups to state-sanctioned athletics teams.

For more than 10 years, Wolcott College Prep High School has been recognized for its innovative approach to learning and student support from the

National Science Foundation, the U.S. Department of Education, and multiple media outlets. Every student who has graduated from the school has been admitted to four-year university and has exceeded the national college persistence rate for all college students, and far exceeded the rate for colleges students with disabilities. But the best measure of any school's success is found in the story of its individual students. Head of School Miriam Pike shared with us the story of James, a student who was changed because a group of educators decided to rethink school.

When James entered Wolcott College Prep High School at the start of ninth grade, he did not know what to expect. He came from a private school where he struggled to learn due to the school's inability to meet his learning needs. James had dyslexia with ADHD, and was described as personable, friendly, eager to learn, and an innovative thinker with multiple interests. He struggled significantly with reading, spelling, and attentional regulation. He was also stressed by school and in need of intensive outside tutoring to reteach and support his learning from school. This interfered with his ability to fully participate in extracurriculars and social activities and created a high stress environment for him.

At Wolcott College Prep, James took a rigorous course schedule and was taught to his strengths while enhancing his skills, learning effective strategies, and learning supports through his content area and Learning Strategies classes. He succeeded in his courses and achieved his self-designed learning plan goals while participating in volleyball, robotics, student council and more.

When James graduated from Wolcott College Prep, he still had dyslexia and ADHD. However, many of his skills rose to the Superior range, while his accommodated silent reading comprehension was in the High Average. He gained the content knowledge, skills, and strategies to learn and advocate while gaining the confidence to succeed. As a result, James was selected to give the student address at his Wolcott graduation ceremony where he described his journey.

"Before the pandemic, before online learning, before several schedule changes, a boy walked into his new high school not knowing the journey he was about to undertake. His knees were weak, and his arms were heavy. Sometimes this journey seemed frustrating and even hopeless.

But at this new school something was different. Before, he would sit in the back of the classroom hoping not to be seen. But they saw him. Before, he didn't want to say the wrong thing, but they asked him his thoughts and opinions. And before, he didn't want to read aloud, but

(Continued)

(Continued)

here, they challenged him to grow and to learn without fear. The mission at Wolcott College Prep is self-awareness, confidence, and resilience so that students thrive. So simply put, that little boy could take a deep breath, relax, and be able to learn without failure."

"Nelson Mandela said, 'I learned that courage is not the absence of fear, but triumph over it.' And now four years later that little boy is standing here reading aloud in public."

"Graduates, as we were one step away from turning those tassels, I commend you. I commend you for your hard work over these last four years. I applaud you for your daily effort and drive. For every essay, every homework assignment, and every presentation, I say bravo. For taking this opportunity to dig deep and find out the learner that you are. I can proudly stand here today and say to those kids in the back of the classroom, they have the courage to stand out. They can go and be confident and let their light shine. Those kids who were afraid to say something wrong, they have the courage to give an answer. They are able to find their truth and let their thoughts be known. And those kids whose palms were sweating because they didn't want to read aloud, they have the courage to grasp their destiny.

Now fellow graduates, it is time for us to show the world how smart and resilient we are. Our creativity, our ideas and our passion are the building blocks to the best future and will help us write one. As Kendrick Lamar said, 'Reach for the moon and even if you fall short, you will land among the stars.'"

James is currently attending a highly selective university. He adjusted well to college and rose to the academic challenge using all Wolcott College Prep's tools. He joined the finance club by invitation and played for the men's club volleyball team. In addition, he was selected to join an international business seminar through a school of business in Dubai. Most recently, James and his parents sent a note to the school, thanking them for all they had done for him, along with a financial gift to be used to help future students like James.

CONCLUSION

Our goal for this book is to lay out a blueprint for the schools we need right now, in the midst of a mental health crisis and when schools are at a crossroads for what they will look like in the 21st century. In the aftermath of a global pandemic, there is an opportunity to rethink schools through the lens of mental health and wellness. This won't diminish academic learning. Instead, as we have argued, it will be enhanced. More importantly, the mental and physical health of students and staff will be equal to the academic mission. The content of schooling will finally include all dimensions of a healthy school: academic, social, emotional, physical. This whole child, whole school philosophy will provide every individual what they need while lifting up the entire school community.

In each chapter, we've asked you to pause and reflect along the way, thinking about yourself, your students, your school, and your community as a way to think through all the different ways you can create a more mentally healthy school. It is now time to step back to see the big picture, to "play the whole ball-game" of re-creating your school. In the Appendix, we've provided you with a Mental Health Action Plan Template as a tool to organize these conversations with the stakeholders in your school and community as you develop your own action plan that is customized for you.

This book has traced a number of "through-lines" that represent important mental models that are essential to a mentally healthy school. Some have been explicit and tied into the structure of the book, like the three MTSS tiers, the focus on prevention rather than intervention, a whole school systems-thinking philosophy, and the centering of social and emotional learning. Others have been explicated through strategies. For example, using restorative practices and circles as a way to develop better relationships between students and a culture of caring throughout the school. As with good teaching and learning, there is a strong connection between theory and practice, between what we do and why we do it. School leaders and educators must try to keep both in mind at all times as we make decisions to improve the lives of students, staff, and families. We hope these ideas will guide you as you embark on this most important of journeys.

CREATING YOUR MENTAL HEALTH ACTION PLAN

Take some time to work with your school-based team to think through the following elements of your comprehensive Mental Health Action Plan. The full plan template is located in Appendix A.

Evaluation and Feedback

1. How do we evaluate our Mental Health Action Plan?

2. How do we collect feedback on our school and our plan?

3. How often do we evaluate our plan?

4. How is the plan used to continuously improve wellness, mental health, and SEL-related systems, practices, and policies?

REFERENCES

Afterschool Alliance. (2020). *America After 3PM special report: Afterschool in communities of concentrated poverty*. Afterschool Alliance. http://www.afterschoolalliance.org/AA3PM/ Concentrated_Poverty.pdf

American Institutes for Research. (2015). *Supporting social and emotional development through quality afterschool programs*. American Institutes for Research. http://https:// www.air.org/sites/default/files/downloads/report/Social-and-Emotional-DevelopmentAfter- school-Programs.pdf

Browning, M. H. E. M., & Rigolon, A. (2019). School green space and its impact on academic performance: A systematic literature review. *International Journal of Environmental Research and Public Health*, 16(3), 429. https://doi.org/10.3390/ijerph16030429

Centers for Disease Control (CDC). (2022). *Schools start too early*. https://www.cdc.gov/sleep/ features/schools-start-too-early.html

Feldman, J. (2019). *Grading for equity: What it is why it matters and how it can transform schools and classrooms*. Corwin.

Filardo, M., Vincent, J. M., & Sullivan, K. (2019). How crumbling school facilities perpetuate inequality. *Phi Delta Kappan*, 100(8), 27–31. https://kappanonline.org/how-crumbling-sch ool-facilities-perpetuate-inequality-filardo-vincent-sullivan/

Fullan, M. (2006). The future of educational change: System thinkers in action. *Journal of Educational Change*, 7, 113–122. https://doi.org/10.1007/s10833-006-9003-9

Hammond, Z. (2015). *Culturally responsive teaching and the brain: Promoting authentic engagement and rigor among culturally and linguistically diverse students*. Corwin.

Horton, T. (2021). Nature connections and social emotional learning. In *Evolutionary and Ecological Approaches to Health and Development*. Northwestern University.

Jackson, C. K., Rockoff, J. E., & Staiger, D. O. (2014). Teacher effects and teacher-related policies. *Annual Review of Economics*, 6, 801–825. https://doi.org/10.1146/annurev-eco- nomics-080213-040845

Knight, J., & Learning Forward. (2013). *High-impact instruction: A framework for great teaching*. Corwin.

Learning Policy InstituteTurnaround for Children. (2021). *Design principles for schools: Putting the science of learning and development into action*. https://k12.designprincip les.org/

Mayo Clinic Health System. (2021, May 28). *Children and screen time: How much is too much?* https://www.mayoclinichealthsystem.org/hometown-health/speaking-of-health/chil- dren-and-screen-time

McCombs, J., Whitaker, A., & Yoo, P. (2017). *The value of out-of-school time programs*. Rand Corporation. https://www.rand.org/content/dam/rand/pubs/perspectives/PE200/PE 267/RAND_PE267.pdf

Moser, W. (2016). Does green space make better students? *Chicago Magazine*. https://www. chicagomag.com/city-life/march-2016/green-space-schools/

Oakes, J., Maier, A., & Daniel, J. (2017). *Community schools: An evidence-based strategy for equitable school improvement*. Learning Policy Institute.

Owens, J., & Adolescent Sleep Working Group, and Committee on Adolescence. (2014). Insufficient sleep in adolescents and young adults: An update on causes and consequences. *Pediatrics*, 134(3), e921–e932. 10.1542/peds.2014-1696

Paul, M. (2023). More green spaces linked to slower biological aging. *Northwestern Now.* https://news.northwestern.edu/stories/2023/06/more-green-spaces-linked-to-slower-biological-aging/?linkId=223408369

Perkins, D. (2009). *Making learning whole: How seven principles of teaching can transform education.* Jossey-Bass.

Ruder, D. (June 19, 2019). *Screen time and the brain: Digital devices can interfere with everything from sleep to creativity.* Harvard Medical School News & Research. https://hms.harvard.edu/news/screen-time-brain

Schneider, M. (2002). Do school facilities affect academic outcomes? National Clearinghouse for Educational Facilities.

Schultz, B. (2023). *To improve kids' mental health, some schools start later.* Associated Press. https://apnews.com/article/school-start-times-pandemic-be81b0f5cb2b68fad3ce0a22dfd8ac1f

Senge, P. (2006). *The fifth discipline: The art and practice of the learning organization.* Random House Books.

Stiggins, R. (2024). *Give our students the gift of confidence.* Corwin.

West, D. (2023, May 23). *Social media can put young people in danger, U.S. surgeon general warns.* NPR. https://www.npr.org/2023/05/23/1177626373/u-s-surgeon-general-vivek-murthy-warns-about-the-dangers-of-social-media-to-kids

APPENDIX A

·····································

MENTAL HEALTH ACTION PLAN

PURPOSE OF THE MENTAL HEALTH ACTION PLAN

This document aligns with the content of *The Schools We Need Now*, where you will find additional details and organizing concepts to use as you assess, implement and coordinate a Mental Health Action Plan. We believe that the mental health and wellness of your school are essential and that when students' mental health and emotional needs are met, they are more likely to succeed in school. This document is designed to be a needs assessment and action plan, one that can align, integrate and address the needs, resources and steps to ensure that every student has the opportunity to succeed in your school.

SCHOOL VISION, MISSION, MOTTO

1. Our school's vision is

| |
| |
| |

2. Our school's mission is

| |
| |
| |

3. Our school's motto is

```

```

VISION AND MISSION: OPERATIONALIZING OUR CORE VALUES AND BELIEFS

What one sentence represents your school's or district's core values or beliefs about each of the following? Identify at least one specific program, practice, or service that represents your core values or beliefs in that area:

- Children _____
- Teachers _____
- Staff _____
- Parents _____
- Teaching _____
- Learning _____
- Assessment _____
- Behavior _____
- Mental health _____
- Equity _____
- Community _____
- Relationships _____

CURRENT CONTEXT: DATA AND NEED

1. What is the story of our school?

```

```

2. Who are we? What are our needs? What are our strengths?

COMMUNITY CONTEXT

1. Demographics (total population, age, race, ethnicity, gender, economic, etc.)

2. What is our local community context?

3. Protective factors (characteristics of our school and community that are positive)

4. Assets (current resources that support students, staff, and families)

5. Risk factors (characteristics of our school or community that may have a negative impact on students, staff, or families)

```


```

6. Challenges (specific forces, situations, or barriers that have a negative impact on our school)

```


```

7. What do we consider to be the biggest, most critical mental health or social/emotional need in our school? What does our school need the most help with to improve our mental health? What's missing?

```


```

EXISTING SCHOOL STRUCTURES

1. How are we organized?

```


```

2. What structures do we rely on to accomplish our mission?

```


```

3. What processes drive our organization or hold us back?

```


```

4. What are our policies and practices as stated in print? How do they address mental health? What's missing? Unclear? Inconsistent?

```


```

5. Is mental health a part of our overall wellness strategy? Where do we explicitly and intentionally address mental health and wellness? Do we have an All-School Wellness team?

```


```

PREVENTION AND INTERVENTION

MTSS/RtI: An Integrated Approach With a Continuum of Care

1. How have we structured our school around academics, behavior, and mental health?

```


```

2. What is our "continuum of care"?

```


```

3. In what ways are we "trauma informed"?

```
┌─────────────────────────────────────────────────────────┐
│                                                           │
│                                                           │
│                                                           │
│                                                           │
└─────────────────────────────────────────────────────────┘
```

PREVENTION AND EARLY INTERVENTION PLAN: TIER 1

1. What are we doing for <u>all</u> students?

```
┌─────────────────────────────────────────────────────────┐
│                                                           │
│                                                           │
│                                                           │
│                                                           │
│                                                           │
└─────────────────────────────────────────────────────────┘
```

2. How do we develop culture?

```
┌─────────────────────────────────────────────────────────┐
│                                                           │
│                                                           │
│                                                           │
│                                                           │
│                                                           │
└─────────────────────────────────────────────────────────┘
```

3. How do we get to know each individual?

```
┌─────────────────────────────────────────────────────────┐
│                                                           │
│                                                           │
│                                                           │
│                                                           │
└─────────────────────────────────────────────────────────┘
```

4. How do we build relationships?

```
┌─────────────────────────────────────────────────────────┐
│                                                           │
│                                                           │
│                                                           │
│                                                           │
└─────────────────────────────────────────────────────────┘
```

5. How do we measure school climate?

6. How regularly do we collect and analyze school climate data?

7. How do we use school climate data to drive policy decisions, structures, and processes?

8. How do we offer academic support <u>in</u> classes?

9. How do we offer academic support <u>outside</u> of classes?

10. How do we offer physical health support?

11. How do we offer social and emotional support?

12. How is SEL integrated in our academic program? Cocurricular and extracurricular activities? Athletics?

13. Do we have foundational support and a plan for SEL that strengthens <u>adult</u> capacity and competence and promotes SEL for all students?

14. How do we approach student behavior?

15. Do we have restorative justice practices in our school culture?

16. What would it take for us to change the mindset and skillset of our staff to a restorative justice approach?

```
┌─────────────────────────────────────────────────────────────┐
│                                                               │
│                                                               │
│                                                               │
│                                                               │
│                                                               │
└─────────────────────────────────────────────────────────────┘
```

PREVENTION AND INTERVENTION PLAN: TIER 2

1. What programs or resources do we have that address the following:

   * Stress _____

   * Emotion _____

   * Anxiety _____

   * Crisis and Trauma _____

   * Grief and Loss _____

   * Transitions _____

2. How do we know a student is struggling in or out of school? What are the signs?

```
┌─────────────────────────────────────────────────────────────┐
│                                                               │
│                                                               │
│                                                               │
│                                                               │
│                                                               │
└─────────────────────────────────────────────────────────────┘
```

3. What staff development programs do we have to ensure that staff know how to recognize early signs and symptoms of mental health concerns?

```
┌─────────────────────────────────────────────────────────────┐
│                                                               │
│                                                               │
│                                                               │
│                                                               │
│                                                               │
└─────────────────────────────────────────────────────────────┘
```

4. How do we screen for early identification of potential problems and student concerns?

```
┌─────────────────────────────────────────────────────────────┐
│                                                               │
│                                                               │
│                                                               │
│                                                               │
│                                                               │
└─────────────────────────────────────────────────────────────┘
```

5. What are some interventions we can try to support people who are struggling?

6. How and where are we teaching coping, resiliency, and trauma response?

7. How do we support and empathize staff and teacher wellness?

8. Do we engage and include students as leaders, problem solvers, and decision-makers in the process of addressing mental health?

9. What community partnerships do we have in place with organizations and institutions? What's the referral process and procedure?

10. How do we support parents in their development?

11. How do we define *trauma-informed practice*?

PREVENTION AND INTERVENTION PLAN: TIER 3

1. Do we have suicide prevention, intervention, and postvention plans, procedures, and policies?

2. What information and resources do we rely on related to more severe mental illnesses, such as depression, nonsuicidal noninjury, eating disorders, suicidal ideation, and adverse childhood trauma?

3. What prevention and interventions do we engage in to support students and staff who are grappling with Tier 3 issues?

4. How do we deal with stigma related to serious mental health issues?

CRISIS RESPONSE PLAN

Crisis plans are living documents and crisis management is a continuous process. A good plan is never finished.

1. What is our crisis response plan?

2. Where is it stored?

3. Do we regularly edit and practice it? If yes, how often? If no, what are the barriers?

4. What are its strengths and weaknesses?

5. Who is on our crisis team and are the roles and tasks clearly defined?

EVALUATION AND FEEDBACK

1. How do we evaluate our Mental Health Action Plan?

2. How do we collect feedback on our school and our plan?

3. How often do we evaluate our plan?

4. How is the plan used to continuously improve wellness, mental health, and SEL-related systems, practices, and policies?

INDEX

Ableism, 46, 129

Academic learning, 6, 7, 31, 57–59, 164

Acute trauma events, 76

Addiction, 115, 133

Adkins, A. M., 9–12

Adult behavior, 96

Adverse childhood experiences (ACE), 69

Afterschool Alliance, 156

All-School Wellness Team, 56

American Psychological Association (APA), 1, 73

Amygdala, 49, 71, 71 (figure)

Anne Marie's Law, 122, 160

Anti-bullying programs, 95–96

Anti-Defamation League, 96

Anxiety, 15, 69, 110
  definition, 74
  depression and, 111–113
  disorders, 74, 75, 112
  school refusal, 75–76
  stress, 111
  symptoms of, 74–75

Bandura, A., 50

Behavior management, 94

Belonging, 144–145

Bloom, B., 41

Brain, 49–50
  amygdala, 71
  hippocampus, 71
  work in progress, 72–73

Bridges transition program, 132

Brown, B., 98

Buddy Benches, 96

Burke-Harris, N., 125

Calming Corner, 85

CDC-Kaiser Permanente Adverse Childhood Experiences (ACE) Study, 125

Centers for Disease Control (CDC), 1, 74, 125
  anxiety, 74
  depression, 112
  suicide, 118
  Youth Risk Behavior Survey, 69

Change events, 114

Childhood trauma, 124–126

Circle Forward, 87

Circles, 85–87, 87 (figure)–89 (figure)

Classism, 46

Classroom furniture, 148

Classroom management, 58

Clothesline Project, 95

Coates, T. -N., 98

Cognitive Behavioral Intervention for Trauma in Schools (CBITS), 94

Cognitive functions, 71

Cognitive learning, 57–59

Collaboration, 45, 99, 159

Collaborative for Academic, Social, and Emotional Learning (CASEL), 52

Collective efficacy, 50–51

Comer, J., 31, 52, 144

CommonSense.org, 150

Communication, 75, 111, 116, 159

Community schools, 42, 158

Comorbidity, 108, 110

Compassion, 27
  fatigue, 81

Comprehensive, 143

Conduct disorders, 123

Conflict resolution, 86

Continuum of care, 3, 4, 25–28, 26 (figure)
  components of, 26
  comprehensive, 27

Co-occurring conditions, 110

Cooperative learning, 16, 152

Coping, 50, 51, 68, 110
    adaptive behaviors, 75
    resiliency and, 52, 73
    traumatic event, 77
Cortisol, 71, 74
Coteaching, 10
The Courage to Teach, 23
COVID-19 pandemic, 1, 2, 41,
    80, 99, 145
    mental health crisis, 15
    social isolation, 42, 44
Crisis response, 136–137, 140
Culture of caring, 22–25, 42
Culture of learning, 21
Curriculum, 46, 53, 55, 132, 150–151
Cyberbullying, 48

Decision-making, 52, 53, 151
Deficit models, 4, 47
Dependence, 115
Depression, 15, 75
    anxiety and, 111–113
    mental and physical health issues, 112
Design Principles for Schools, 150
Dewey, J., 17, 145
*Diagnostic and Statistical Manual of Mental
    Disorders*, 5th ed (DSM-5), 123, 126
Dialectical behavioral therapy (DBT), 94,
    118, 131
Digital citizenship, 150
DiMartino, J., 9, 10, 12
Disability, 129
Discrimination, 46
Disordered eating, 117
Disruptive behavior disorders, 123–124
Disruptive impulse control, 123
Distress, 82–84
Duckworth, A., 50
Dweck, C., 50, 98
Dysregulation, 79, 82

Eating disorders, 117
Emoji cloud, 69
Emotional health, 21
Emotional learning, 7, 10
Emotions, 73, 112
Engagement, 144
Equity, 127–128
Erika's Lighthouse, 134, 135
Evans, A., 1
Evans, S. W., 128

Family Action Network (FAN), 98
Fight–flight–freeze response, 49, 70,
    71, 79, 82
Formative assessment, 153

Gardner, H., 98
Golden Apple Foundation, 151
Gorman, A., 85
Grandin, T., 98
Grief, loss and, 80–81

Hammond, Z., 10
Hattie, J., 51
Healthy food, 55
Helplessness, 76
Herbert Akins Road Middle School, 9, 11
Hippocampus, 71
Homelessness, 25
Horton, T., 147

Identity development, 45, 46
Identity formation, 45
Impulsivity, 121
Individualized education plans (IEPs), 68
Individuals with Disabilities Act
    (IDEA), 28
Instructional coaching, 152
Instructional time, maximizing, 58
Internalized behaviors
    anxiety, 74–76
    brain, 72–73, 72 (figure)
    stress, 70–71, 71 (figure), 73
    trauma, 76–77
    Window of Tolerance, 78–79, 78 (figure)
Intersectionality, 46
Isolation, 80–81

*Journal of the American Medical
    Association*, 15

Kendi, I., 98

Ladson-Billings, G., 47
Learning, 147. *See also* Social and emotional
    learning (SEL)
    academic, 57–59
    classroom management, 58
    cognitive, 57–59
    cooperative, 46, 152
    coping skills, 75
    neuroscience, 50
    physical, 54–56

project-based, 152
student-centered, 152
technology, 48
whole-school approach, 21
Lewis, J., 98
The Lighthouse Curriculum, 135
Loneliness, 80–81
Love, B. L., 31

Malleability, 72, 73
Mangoes, 94
Maslow, A., 41
Maslow's hierarchy of needs, 41, 41 (figure)
McLellan, J., 69
Mediation, 11
Medical model, 3, 4
Mental disorder, 108
Mental health
    anxiety, 112
    definition of, 16
    healthy development, 4
    importance, in schools, 2–4, 3 (figure)
    medical model of, 108
    mental models and, 15–31
    multitiered systems of support, 28
    problem, 107
    rethinking technology and, 149–150
    substance use, 115–116
Mental Health Action Plan (MHAP),
    3, 7–9, 15
    community context, 32–33, 173–174
    comprehensive, 160–162
    core values and beliefs, 13, 172
    crisis response plan, 182–183
    data and needs, 32, 172–173
    evaluation and feedback, 166–167, 183
    existing school structures, 174–175
    prevention and intervention, 34, 175–176
    purpose of, 171
    school's mission, 13, 171–172
    school's motto, 13, 171–172
    school structures, 33–34
    school's vision, 13, 171–172
    Tier 1, 62–63, 176–179
    Tier 2, 101–102, 179–181
    Tier 3, 139–140, 181–182
Mental Health Hygiene Plan, 99
Mental illness, 15, 44
    deficit models of, 3
    definition, 107–109
    equity and, 127–128

medical models of, 3
Mental models, 16
    continuum of care, 25–27
    culture of caring, 23–25
    Mental Health Action Plan, 30–31
    mental health, thinking differently about,
        27–28
    multitiered systems of support, 28–29
    systems thinking approach, 20–23
    whole-child approach, 17–20, 18 (figure)
MHAP. *See* Mental Health Action Plan
    (MHAP)
Mind–body–brain connection, 77
Mindful Moment, 154
Mindful Mondays, 85
Mindfulness, 48, 84–85, 87
Mirror neurons, 50
Muhammad, G., 47, 128
Multi-Tiered Systems of Support (MTSS), 3,
    8, 26, 28–29, 38, 67, 68, 122

National Association of Anorexia Nervosa
    and Associated Disorders, 117
National Association of Mental Illness
    (NAMI), 1, 108, 117
National School Climate Center, 24
National Sleep Foundation, 56
Nervous disorder, 74
Neurodivergence, 128
Neurodiversity, 128–129
Neuroplasticity, 50, 72
Neuroscience, 49, 50
Nonsuicidal self-injury, 117

Observable characteristics, 123
Obsessive compulsive disorder, 110
One-size-fits-all model, 57

Palmer, P., 23
Parasympathetic nervous system, 71
Peace Room, 85
Peer Helping, 39, 94–95
Peer mediation, 94–95
Peer Mentoring, 39, 94–95
Peer tutoring, 94–95
Perkins, D., 143
Physical health, 42, 56
Physical learning, wellness and, 54–56
Physical safety, 42
Physical violence, 77
Physical well-being, 27, 54, 56

Pike, M., 47, 128
Pink, D., 98
Plasticity, 72
Positionality, 4–8
Positive Behavioral Interventions and
    Supports (PBIS), 28
Posttraumatic stress disorder
    (PTSD), 110, 126
Pranis, K., 87, 90
Prefrontal cortex, 71
Prevention tool kit, 40
Professional development, 83
Professional learning communities
    (PLCs), 51
Project-based learning, 152
Protective mechanism, 70
Psychological safety, 43
Psychological violence, 77
Psychological well-being, 56
Psychosocial problems, prevention of, 4

Racism, 46
REACHING Act, 160
Redman, R., 53, 54
Relationship-building, 52
Resiliency, 52, 73
Response to intervention (RTI), 28, 38
Restorative discipline, 89–91, 90 (figure)
Restorative justice approach, 86
Restorative practices, 11, 89–91, 90 (figure)
Rethinking
    after-school activities, 156–157
    assessment, 150–153
    curriculum, 150–151
    instruction, 150–151
    organization of a school, 145–146
    physical building, 147–149
    school context and community assets,
        157–160
    teachers and instruction, 151–152
    technology and mental health, 149–150
    transitions, 153–156

Sadness, 112
School climate, 24
School culture, 24
School refusal
    Tier 2, 75–76
    Tier 3, 113–114
School relationships, 10
School resource officer (SRO), 10

School safety, 10
School staff expertise, 130–131
Screen addiction, 48
Screen time, 49
Secondary trauma, 92
Self-awareness, 4, 52, 54, 79
Self-control, 123
Self-efficacy, 50–51
Self-harm, 117–118
Self-management, 51, 52, 54, 79
Self-reflection, 4, 7, 79
Self-regulation, 79
Service learning, 152, 157
Sexism, 46
Seyle, H., 70
Shock, denial and, 77
Short-term memory, 71
Siegel, D., 78
Sleep health, 56
Small groups
    Tier 2, 93–94
    Tier 3, 131–132
Social and emotional learning (SEL), 7, 39,
    40, 52–54, 69, 79, 107
Social awareness, 52
Social connection, 42
Social isolation, 42, 44
Social learning, 7, 10
Social location, 4
Social media, 48–49, 149, 150
Social worker, 5
Societal changes, 114
Steinberg, L., 52
Stephenson, B., 98
Stereotypes, 43–44
Stiggins, R., 153
Stigmas, 43–44
Storytelling, 87
Streedain, D., 144
StrengthenU, 69
Stress, 69
    anxiety, 111
    definition, 70
    impact of, 73
Stressors, 70
Stress response, 41, 70, 71, 73, 77
Student activities, 96–97
Student-centered classroom, 152
Student-centered curriculum, 162
Student-centered learning, 152
Student clubs, 96–97

Substance Abuse and Mental Health Services Administration (SAMSHA), 127
Substance use, 115–116
Suicidal behavior, 119
Suicidal ideation, 1, 118–119
Suicide, 1, 118, 120–121
    attempt, 119
    definitions, 119
    distinctions, 119
    intervention, 121–123
Systems thinking approach, 20–23, 143
    cognitive, 21
    cultural, 22
    emotional, 22
    environmental, 22
    moral, 22
    physical, 21
    social, 21
    spiritual, 22

Teacher training, 151
Technology, 48–49
Tier 1, 29, 70
    academic and cognitive learning, 57–59
    body, teaching about, 49–50
    brain, teaching about, 49–50
    collective efficacy, 50–51
    diversity, equity, and inclusion, 46–47
    early intervention, 39–40
    environmental risk, 47–48
    foundation of, 60–61
    identity, 45–46
    mind, teaching about, 49–50
    physical learning and wellness, 54–56
    prevention, 39–40
    protective factors, 47–48
    relationships and community, disconnection from, 44–45
    safety first, 41–43
    screeners, 68–69
    self-efficacy, 50–51
    social and emotional learning (SEL), 52–54
    social media, 48–49
    stereotypes, 43–44
    stigma, 43–44
    technology, 48–49
    universal, challenges, 38–39, 41
Tier 2, 29
    anti-bullying programs, 95–96
    anxiety, 74–76

brain, work in progress, 72–73
circles, 85–87, 87 (figure)–89 (figure)
distress, 82–84
grief, 80–81
healthy and well-regulated staff, 98–99
internalized behaviors, 70–79
interventions, 67, 68, 82–84
isolation, 80–81
issues, 80–81
loneliness, 80–81
loss, 80–81
mindfulness, 84–85
parent/family education, programs, and engagement, 97–98
Peer Helping, 94–95
peer mediation, 94–95
Peer Mentoring, 94–95
peer tutoring, 94–95
school refusal, 75–76
screeners, 68–69
small groups, 93–94
strategies, 82–84
stress, 70–71, 73
student activities and clubs, 96–97
student behavior and discipline, 89–91, 90 (figure)
teachers, 82
trauma, 76–77
trauma-informed care, 92–93
Window of Tolerance, 78–79, 78 (figure)
Tier 3, 29, 106
    anxiety, 111–113
    Bridges transition program, 132
    childhood trauma, 124–126
    community organizations and resources, 134–135
    comorbidity, 110
    connects to Tier 1 and Tier 2, 106–108
    crisis response, 136–137
    definition, 106–108
    depression, 111–113
    disordered eating, 117
    disruptive behavior disorders, 123–124
    equity and mental illness, 127–128
    intervention, 129–137
    mental illness, 108–109
    neurodiversity, 128–129
    parent and family support, 133
    prevention, 129–137
    school refusal, 113–114

school staff expertise and training, 130–131

self-harm, 117–118

small groups, 131–132

substance use, 115–116

suicidal ideation, 118–120

suicide intervention, 120–123

transitions, 114–115

Transitions, 114–115, 153–156

Trauma, 69

childhood, 124–126

definition, 76

events, 76, 77

individual, 76

secondary, 92

Trauma-informed care, 92–93

Unearthing Joy, 128

Universal Design for Learning (UDL), 57, 58

Universal Tier 1 approach, 38–39

U.S. Department of Education, 42

Vaping, 115

Violence, 77, 120

Virtual calm corner, 85

Vulnerability, 76

Well-being, 15, 76, 109

mental health and, 150

physical, 29, 54, 56

psychological, 56

Whole-child approach, 17–20

cognitive, 18

cultural, 19

emotional, 18–19

environmental, 19

morals/ethics, 19

physical, 18

social, 18

spiritual, 19

Window of Tolerance, 78–79, 78 (figure)

Wolcott College Prep, 162–164

Working memory, 71

World Health Organization, 15, 16

Youth Risk Behavior Surveillance System (YRBSS), 109

Zero-tolerance policies, 59, 91

A Sage Company

CORWIN HAS ONE MISSION: to enhance education through intentional professional learning.

We build long-term relationships with our authors, educators, clients, and associations who partner with us to develop and continuously improve the best evidence-based practices that establish and support lifelong learning.